WOMEN'S PACs

REAL POLITICS IN AMERICA

Series Editor: Paul S. Herrnson, *University of Maryland*

The books in this series bridge the gap between academic scholarship and the popular demand for knowledge about politics. They illustrate empirically supported generalizations from original research and the academic literature using examples taken from the legislative process, executive branch decision making, court rulings, lobbying efforts, election campaigns, political movements, and other areas of American politics. The goal of the series is to convey the best contemporary political science research has to offer in ways that will engage individuals who want to know about real politics in America.

WOMEN'S PACS

ABORTION AND ELECTIONS

Christine L. Day
University of New Orleans

Charles D. Hadley
University of New Orleans

PEARSON

Prentice Hall

UPPER SADDLE RIVER, NEW JERSEY 07458

Library of Congress Cataloging-in-Publication Data

Day, Christine L.
    Women's PACs: abortion and elections/Christine L. Day, Charles D. Hadley.
        p. cm.—(Real politics in America)
    Includes bibliographical references and index.
    ISBN 0-13-117448-7
    1. Women in politics—United States.   2. Political action committees—United
States.   I. Hadley, Charles D.   II. Title.   III. Series.

    HQ1236.5.U6D39   2005
    320'.082—dc22

                                                            2004016570

Editorial Director: Charlyce Jones Owen
Acquisitions Editor: Glenn Johnston
Editorial Assistant: Suzanne Remore
Marketing Manager: Kara Kindstrom
Marketing Assistant: Jennifer Lang
Prepress and Manufacturing Buyer: Sherry Lewis
Cover Art Director: Jayne Conte
Interior Design: John P. Mazzola
Cover Design: Bruce Kenselaar
Composition/Full-Service Project Management: Kari Callaghan Mazzola and John P.
    Mazzola
Printer/Binder: Courier Companies, Inc.
Cover Printer: Phoenix Color Corp.

This book was set in 10/12 Palatino.

Real Politics in America
Series Editor: Paul S. Herrnson

Pearson Education LTD.
Pearson Education Singapore, Pte. Ltd
Pearson Education, Canada, Ltd
Pearson Education–Japan
Pearson Education Australia PTY, Limited

Pearson Education North Asia Ltd
Pearson Educación de Mexico, S.A. de C.V.
Pearson Education Malaysia, Pte. Ltd
Pearson Education, Upper Saddle River, NJ

10 9 8 7 6 5 4 3 2 1
ISBN 0-13-117448-7

For Steve
and
for Nathaniel

CONTENTS

CHAPTER 3

ATTRIBUTES AND ACTIVITIES OF THE MAJOR CONTRIBUTORS   32

CHAPTER 4

POLITICAL ATTITUDES: CONFLICT AND UNITY AMONG
CONTRIBUTORS   48

CHAPTER 5

FEMALE AND MALE CONTRIBUTORS: A GENDER GAP?   64

ACKNOWLEDGMENTS

Many people helped with this project from early survey design to final book production, and we are grateful to all. Robert Biersack of the Federal Election Commission was very helpful in compiling the FEC data on which we based the mailing lists for the contributor survey. M. Kent Jennings kindly shared ideas from the questionnaire for his own NAMES Project Volunteer Survey. Research assistants George S. Chambers, Ursula Daxecker, Megan Duffy Brown Hubbard, Hannes Richter, Sabine Schafer, and Catherine R. Setzer helped us organize the data, mail surveys, and track down information both here and at the FEC office in Washington, D.C. Kerry Hutchinson, Regina Pirolozzi, and Nicole Scott provided invaluable administrative assistance.

Several people read early chapter drafts or papers related to this project, enabling us to shape and improve it with their ideas: Lisa A. Baldez, Lee Ann Banaszak, Robert Biersack, Barbara C. Burrell, Rosalyn Cooperman, Victoria A. Farrar-Myers, John C. Green, Eric S. Heberlig, and Laura R. Woliver. Laurel Elder of Hartwick College, Susan Johnson of the University of Wisconsin–Whitewater, and Kendra Stewart of Eastern Kentucky University also read the entire manuscript and offered invaluable advice. *Real Politics in America* series editor Paul S. Herrnson encouraged us to bring our research together in a book, offering helpful and insightful suggestions that made this a far better book. Members of the Prentice Hall editorial staff offered friendly and efficient professional assistance; we give special thanks to Glenn Johnston, Beth Mejia, Charlyce Jones Owen, and Suzanne Remore.

A portion of the material in Chapter 5 appeared previously in our article "Gender, Feminism, and Partisanship among Women's PAC Contributors," by Christine L. Day, Charles D. Hadley, and Megan Duffy Brown, in *Social Science Quarterly* 82 (December 2001): 687–700, and it is used with permission of Blackwell Publishers. Megan Duffy Brown [Hubbard]'s senior honors thesis became the basis for the article she co-authored with us, and it also became the basis for much of Chapter 5. We are grateful for Megan's able assistance at several stages of our research in addition to her work on what is now Chapter 5.

The College of Liberal Arts at the University of New Orleans provided funding for the Women's PAC Contributor Survey and related research through a series of faculty research and faculty development grants. The Washington Academic Internship Program of the John Glenn Institute for Public Service and Public Policy at The Ohio State University, directed by Elizabeth M. Boles, and the Center for American Politics and Citizenship at the University of Maryland, directed by Paul S. Herrnson, generously provided office space, use of facilities, and copious amounts of coffee while Christine was conducting interviews in Washington, D.C.

Finally, we are grateful to the leaders of EMILY's List, The WISH List, and the Susan B. Anthony List, who cheerfully consented to personal interviews, and to the contributors to all three organizations who took the time to respond to our survey.

Christine L. Day
Charles D. Hadley

Introduction

Female politicians, and the women's political action committees (PACs) that support them, are extremely diverse. But together, they are changing the male-dominated face of American politics. By 2004, the number of women in Congress had never surpassed 14 percent. But it was higher than ever before, and it had more than tripled in three decades. Eight women served as state governors, only 16 percent, but also more than ever before. No woman had ever been elected president or vice president, but Democrat Geraldine Ferraro in 1984 had been on a major-party ticket as a vice presidential candidate. Women had increased their representation at every level in every branch of government. Gradually, the political "glass ceiling" that prevents women from achieving parity in politics is beginning to crack.

Introducing Three Women's PACs

Women's PACs, founded by women to raise money primarily or exclusively for female candidates, stand at the nexus of political change and politics as usual: bringing women into positions of power by mastering the political money game. Like female activists and candidates, women's PACs extend across the partisan and ideological spectrum. This book focuses on three of them, reflecting the range of partisan and ideological positions among women's PACs. They are as follows:

> **EMILY's List**, which supports pro-choice Democratic female candidates.[1] EMILY stands for Early Money Is Like Yeast (it makes the dough rise).
>
> **The WISH List**, which supports pro-choice Republican female candidates. WISH stands for Women in the Senate and House.
>
> **The Susan B. Anthony List**, which supports pro-life female candidates and opposes pro-choice female candidates. It is named after the nineteenth-century suffragist and women's rights activist who, according to the organization, was an outspoken critic of abortion.[2]

PACs are dependent on individual contributors who provide the funds used to support the PACs' chosen candidates. These contributors, or more precisely those who give at least $200 during a single election cycle, are the primary focus of this study: Who are the people who give money to these women's PACs, and what are their political attitudes, activities, and goals? To what extent do their priorities conform to those of the three PACs? How do the contributors to EMILY's List, The WISH List, and the Susan B. Anthony List differ from each other, and what do they have in common?[3]

Political contributors, especially those who contribute in the hundreds of dollars or more, comprise a small but influential portion of the voting-age population. Fewer than one-fourth of Americans of voting age contribute to political campaigns, and only about one-third of 1 percent contribute $200 or more in a single election cycle. The contributions from those few individuals who give at least $200 make up about two-thirds of all individual donations to congressional candidates, and more than a third of the total money raised by those candidates.[4] The influence of those large contributors derives from the enormous cost of modern campaigns and from the fact that election outcomes are highly dependent on campaign spending. Nevertheless, despite their importance, and despite the fact that information about large contributors is, by law, available to the public, individual contributors have seldom been surveyed or studied systematically.[5] The literature on PACs from an organizational point of view is voluminous; the literature on people who contribute to those organizations and to candidates is slim.

In addition to filling a gap in knowledge about these contributors, a second motivation for this study is a desire to understand more about women's participation in the game of campaign finance. These three women's PACs are atypical in several ways: The majority of their contributors are women, while most campaign contributors generally are men. They were founded by women, and they support female candidates, in a political world where leadership positions are held overwhelmingly by men. Thus, these PACs would seem on the surface to be driven by feminist concerns: furthering women's equality while eliminating the patriarchal political system. Yet as we shall see, while many of their contributors are indeed strong supporters of feminism, others reject the feminist label, and some are downright hostile to many feminist goals. Naturally we are interested in both the female and the male contributors, and the similarities and variations between them and within each group.

Who are the female candidates funded by these three PACs? A few examples illustrate their diversity.[6]

THE WISH LIST

Jennifer Dunn, Deborah Pryce, and twenty-six other women rode into Congress on the 1992 tidal wave: an unprecedented increase in female representation, leading the media to designate 1992 the "Year of the Woman." Both

Representative Dunn, of Washington state, and Representative Pryce, of Ohio, are Republicans who vote their party's conservative line on a wide range of issues. Their votes against the 1993 Family and Medical Leave Act (FMLA), which requires businesses to grant their employees unpaid leave to care for a newborn baby or ill family member, put them in conflict with feminist groups and most other women in Congress. Still, their perspectives and experiences as women help shape their legislative actions, and they often address political issues in terms of their impact on women, children, and families. Representative Pryce even suggested she had changed her mind on the family and medical leave issue after she spent nearly three months away from the Capitol in 1998, caring for her young daughter who was diagnosed with a rare childhood cancer. Both congresswomen support restrictions on abortion, yet both have been criticized by anti-abortion groups as being too liberal on such issues as federal aid for family planning funds and services. And both received financial support in their campaigns from The WISH List, the pro-choice Republican women's PAC.

The WISH List has supported both candidates against Democratic opposition as well as against pro-life opposition within their own party. Both women were first elected to Congress in 1992 open-seat races. Jennifer Dunn edged out Pam Roach, a Mormon and ardent opponent of abortion, in the primary election before more easily defeating Democratic nominee George Tamblyn. Deborah Pryce ran unopposed in her district's Republican primary election, but only after convincing the county Republican committee to endorse her over other candidate hopefuls who supported abortion rights in at least limited form. After her primary victory, she clarified her own support for abortion rights generally despite her opposition to abortion personally, angering several pro-life activists within the party. In the general election, she defeated both Democratic nominee Richard Cordray and vocal pro-life Republican Linda Reidelbach, who ran as an independent.

THE SUSAN B. ANTHONY LIST

Sue Myrick of North Carolina and Ileana Ros-Lehtinen of Florida, both Republicans, have racked up staunchly conservative records as members of Congress. Yet both have deviated from the mainstream Republican position on a number of issues, albeit in different directions. Representative Ros-Lehtinen, the first Cuban American and the first Hispanic woman elected to Congress, crossed party lines to support the liberal position on some immigration, welfare, labor, and gun-control issues. Representative Myrick, conversely, bucked the party leadership by taking a hard conservative line on several social and economic issues and opposing bipartisan compromise. But the two congresswomen are united in their strong opposition to abortion. Both often assert their views on abortion and other issues by invoking their role as mothers and their commitment to family values. Both received financial assistance from the Susan B. Anthony List, the pro-life women's PAC.

Both women won hard-fought races in their initial, open-seat elections to Congress. The major hurdle for Sue Myrick in 1994 was the five-way Republican primary. After that, she sailed past her runoff opponent, David Balmer, once the news broke that he had falsified his resume, and then she easily defeated Democratic opponent Rory Blake in the heavily Republican district. Ileana Ros-Lehtinen easily beat her primary opponents in the 1989 special election to fill the seat of the late Representative Claude Pepper in a district with an increasingly large majority of Cuban Americans, who tend to vote Republican. Still, she ran a more difficult race against Democratic nominee Gerald Richman, who tried to defeat the Cuban-American candidate by saying the district was "an American seat." After eking out a victory against Richman, her seat became increasingly secure and her campaign war chest became increasingly formidable thanks to the Susan B. Anthony List among other contributors.

EMILY'S LIST

Loretta Sanchez and Debbie Stabenow have a great deal in common. Both are Democrats who defeated conservative Republican incumbents in the 1996 congressional elections. Their strong support for abortion rights, environmental regulation, public education, and organized labor places them in the liberal camp. At the same time, both have developed reputations as moderate pragmatists, especially on fiscal policy matters. Both congresswomen found themselves in the national spotlight early in their congressional careers. In 2000, Representative Stabenow, having served only two terms in Congress, ran for the U.S. Senate and defeated the Republican incumbent, becoming Michigan's first female senator and one of only thirteen women in the U.S. Senate. Two years later, in 2002, Loretta Sanchez's sister Linda Sanchez ran for Congress and won in a newly drawn California district; Loretta and Linda Sanchez then became the first sisters ever to serve together in Congress. Senator Stabenow and the Sanchez sisters received financial assistance from EMILY's List, the pro-choice Democratic women's PAC.

Defeating an incumbent in Congress is a nearly impossible feat, but EMILY's List leaders recognized that both California Representative Robert Dornan and Michigan Representative Dick Chrysler were vulnerable in 1996. Representative Dornan was an outspoken conservative and a passionate opponent of abortion in a district that was becoming increasingly Democratic and increasingly Hispanic, opening the door to a successful challenge from Loretta Sanchez, a daughter of Mexican immigrants who were labor union activists. Representative Chrysler was a first-term Republican congressman in a district that had been held by Democrats for nearly two decades. Michigan Democratic party officials encouraged Debbie Stabenow through an easy primary victory, and organized labor helped her win the general election with its own negative campaign against Representative Chrysler's voting record in Congress. When Representative Stabenow ran for the U.S. Senate in 2000, she defeated yet another pro-life Republican incumbent, Senator Spencer Abraham, whose wife, Jane Abraham, coincidentally, was the president of the Susan B. Anthony List.

CAMPAIGN FINANCE AND THE ROLE OF PACS

Women's PACs operate within the context of myriad rules and regulations governing the financing of federal campaigns, and an even greater variety of state-level campaign finance laws governing state and local elections. Primary objectives of campaign finance laws include limiting the influence of a few wealthy interests over public policy, and requiring public disclosure so that voters know who is funding their candidates. The laws regulate contributions from individuals, interest groups, and political parties.

Interest groups wishing to contribute money to federal candidates must register with the Federal Election Commission (FEC) and, like political party committees and the candidates themselves, they must report their campaign-related financial activity periodically. Although the term "political action committee," or its acronym "PAC," does not actually appear in legislation, it has become widely used to refer to those organizations that are registered with the FEC and that can therefore legally contribute to candidates. This legal framework, codified in the Federal Election Campaign Act of 1974, enables the federal government to keep tabs on political contributions from interest groups, to make those contributions open to public scrutiny, and to enforce the contribution limits for each election cycle. PAC contributions are limited to $5,000 per candidate per election, or up to $15,000 in a single cycle if the candidate runs in a primary, a runoff, and a general election. Individual contributions are limited to $2,000 per candidate per election, or up to $6,000 in a single election cycle. In addition, individual contributors were limited in 2002 to an aggregate total of $95,000 per election cycle, an amount indexed for inflation.[7] State regulations and limits on contributions to candidates in state and local elections vary from state to state, and they are generally less stringent than those at the national level.

Candidates running for Congress typically get more than 90 percent of their campaign money from individual contributors and from PACs. The remaining small amount comes from the major political parties and the candidate's own pocket (the exceptions are those very wealthy candidates who fund most of their own campaigns out-of-pocket). While individual contributions remain the largest source of congressional campaign funds, the proportion coming from PACs has increased steadily since the 1970s, to just over 40 percent for House candidates and somewhat less for Senate candidates.

This breakdown of individual versus PAC contributions, however, probably underestimates the financial impact of interest groups on congressional elections, because PACs can collect individual contributions and forward them directly to candidates. This process, known as "bundling," based on the image of an organization handing over a bundle of checks, permits an organization to apprise a candidate of its involvement and support beyond the group's legal contribution limit. Although groups engaged in bundling—known as "conduit organizations"—must report bundled contributions of $200 or more to the FEC, the donations themselves are recorded as individual, not PAC, contributions in the FEC database, and they are counted against individual, not PAC, contribution limits. Further, PACs need not report individual bundled donations of less than $200 at all. Thus bundling can enhance an interest group's political clout far beyond that suggested in the FEC PAC contribution data. Nevertheless, many PACs choose not to engage in bundling because of the cumbersome reporting requirements and because of the risk of having to send money to candidates not endorsed by the PAC leadership.[8] But EMILY's List, The WISH List, and the Anthony List do bundle contributions, among their various activities in support of female candidates. EMILY's List, in particular, raised bundling to an art form, becoming the most prominent and visible conduit organization by the early 1990s because of the massive amounts of money it raised and channeled to congressional candidates, and serving as a model to other PACs including The WISH List and the Anthony List.

WOMEN'S PACS AND THE FEMINIZATION OF AMERICAN ELECTORAL POLITICS

The fund-raising success of women's PACs is helping female candidates make tremendous inroads in the male bastion of politics. Although women are still grossly underrepresented at all levels of government, their numbers have multiplied as they have learned how to raise the funds needed to win. Studies dating back to the 1980s show that female candidates, controlling for incumbency and party, raise at least as much money on average as male candidates.[9] Virtually every account of women's gains in electoral politics during the 1990s credits women's PACs with much of this success.[10] In addition to contributing money directly and bundling individual donations to candidates, EMILY's List, The WISH List, and the Anthony List also recruit and train potential candidates and provide additional campaign support services. Their main emphasis has been on electing members of Congress, but they are expanding their operations into state politics as well.[11]

As women's PACs have grown and excelled in the field of campaign finance, they have encountered some of the criticisms leveled against many traditional PACs. Detractors charge that women's PACs have become institutionalized and entrenched, touting progressive change while in fact taking fewer risks in supporting outsiders over insiders than they used to take, and focusing excessively on numerical representation at the expense of meaningful transformation of the political system. In short, they operate like "old-girl networks."[12] Still, in an electoral system where PACs overwhelmingly support incumbents over challengers, women's PACs remain relatively more supportive of challengers. Their activities are even more valuable to women than comparable organizational efforts are to men, because female candidates are more dependent on small individual contributions than are men.[13] Thus, women's networks have had to excel, not only to make inroads into heavily male-dominated elective offices, but also to compensate for men's fund-raising advantages among large donors.

Efforts and accomplishments of such magnitude, largely by women on behalf of women, illustrate the importance of electoral politics to the larger movement for women's equality. However, this was not always the case. Leaders of the first-wave women's movement, in the late nineteenth and early twentieth centuries, pushed for suffrage and other reforms including educational opportunity, property rights, and legal protections for divorcees and their children, but they did not generally encourage women to run for political office. While many did advocate increasing women's representation in elective office once suffrage was achieved, their efforts were hampered by divisions over tactics within the movement as well as by its ties to the Progressives' more protectionist agenda.[14]

Movement activists early in the second wave, which began in the 1960s, were more interested in fighting discrimination from the outside than in electing women to office, an endeavor some saw "as tantamount to complicity in an oppressive, male-dominated system."[15] The first organizations focused primarily on the election of women emerged in the early to mid-1970s, and women's PACs expanded tremendously in number, resources, and visibility after the mid-1980s. EMILY's List, founded in 1985, quickly became the queen of all women's PACs in terms of fund-raising success and media attention. The WISH List was founded in 1992 to counterbalance the success enjoyed by EMILY's List in supporting Democratic women, by supporting Republican women. One year later, the Anthony List was founded to counteract the success enjoyed by both organizations in supporting pro-choice women, by supporting pro-life women and opposing pro-choice women. Meanwhile, other women's PACs continued to emerge, and by the early 1990s there were more than fifty state and national PACs contributing primarily or exclusively to female candidates and/or having a predominantly female donor base.[16]

Democratic female candidates have been the main beneficiaries of support from women's PACs overall, as most women's PACs support Democrats primarily or exclusively and disproportionately give Democrats the early money so crucial to campaign success.[17] There are two major, related reasons why this is so. First, as women have only begun to enter electoral politics in significant numbers during the last few decades, the first ones to do so were, almost by definition, feminist activists challenging the traditional patriarchal system. As more women entered the political mainstream, elite and public resistance to female politicians gave way to acceptance and approval, paving the way for even more women, spanning the ideological spectrum, to enter the electoral arena. Nevertheless, liberal feminists have had a head start over non-feminist or antifeminist women in their pursuit and cultivation of financial and other means of support.

Second, women's rights groups early in the second wave were largely nonpartisan, and support for such issues as women's equality and abortion rights cut across party lines. However, over time the major political parties became increasingly polarized around such issues, particularly in the 1980s, so that liberal feminists became a major constituency of the Democratic party while conservative Christians became a major constituency of the Republican party.[18] Thus, most women's rights groups, including women's PACs, have become increasingly aligned with the Democratic party. This confluence of liberal feminism, women's early electoral activism, and Democratic partisanship has contributed to the large size and financial success of EMILY's List.

At the same time, conservative women, aligned naturally with the Republican party, gradually began to enter the electoral arena as well. These include laissez-faire conservative women who generally prefer smaller, noninterventionist government (with a few exceptions, as in the area of national defense), and socially conservative women who prefer a more active government imposing a more traditional social order.[19] The WISH List draws most of its contributors from the former group, while the Anthony List draws from the latter.

Today, then, women across the partisan and ideological spectrum have been mobilized to support women in their quest for public office. Many men, too, contribute money toward the goal of electing more women. But the majority of contributors to all three of the PACs examined here are women: 94 percent in EMILY's List, 90 percent in The WISH List, and 54 percent in the Anthony List. Perhaps it is not surprising that a large majority of people who contribute to these women's PACs are women. But it does reflect a very different gender balance from that of the total population of political contributors in the United States, who are disproportionately male.

GENDER AND PARTICIPATION: A GAP IN GIVING

Women participate in politics at a slightly lower rate than do men. Although the participation gender gap has narrowed in recent decades, and even disappeared for some activities such as voting, women still lag behind in other activities. The difference is especially pronounced with regard to campaign contributions, in part because, once active, women are more likely than men to give of their time, while men are more likely than women to give money.[20] Considering the increasing importance of money in campaigns and the access to policymakers that money can buy, the gender difference is politically significant.

The gender gap is even greater among the large contributors who give $200 or more; about three-fourths of them are men. Further, the Center for Responsive Politics presents evidence that the difference may even be larger than officially reported to the FEC: Because of the legal limits on individual contributions, husbands who have given up to their limit may give more in the name of their wives. Their evidence is based on the fact that men's contributions outweigh women's even more in the "soft money" category—contributions that were not limited by law until 2004.[21]

The reasons for women's lower participation rates are a complex mix of socialization, and situational and structural (primarily socioeconomic) factors: Children are socialized to believe that politics is a man's world; adult women are often situated in the private-domain roles of wife and mother and less involved in the public domain outside the household; and women are less likely than men to have the resources that facilitate participation, such as money, education, and occupational prestige and connections. These three types of factors are interrelated and difficult to separate.[22]

When it comes to making political contributions, however, the answer is much simpler: It is women's relative lack of financial resources that is paramount. Contributing money is exceptional among political activities in that income is by far the most important factor in determining who gives, and how much; it is the activity in which the economically disadvantaged are most underrepresented. If women had the same amount of wealth, and the same amount of control over household finances that men do, researchers conclude, their political contributions also would be nearly equal to men's.[23]

Whatever their wealth or ability, people are more inclined to get involved and give money when they are asked to do so. Men are more likely than women to appeal to others to participate politically; and, when they do make requests or recruit others, they most often approach other men. This applies to contributions as well as to other activities. Thus, mobilization efforts by political activists and elites also help explain the gender gap in participation.[24]

Some feminist scholars contend that many political participation scholars exaggerate gender differences in participation rates. They have done so by emphasizing electoral politics, political parties, and interest groups, while overlooking many of the activities women have long engaged in, such as grassroots community activity, voluntary associations, and social movements.[25] This may be true historically, but more recent research finds that women do not engage disproportionately in local or grassroots politics.[26] Perhaps, a few decades into the second-wave women's movement, well-established institutionalized women's organizations and PACs have become the primary mobilizers of women, substituting to some extent for the ad-hoc grassroots activities of old. Indeed, among large donors—those who donate $200 or more to candidates—women tend to receive at least as many requests for contributions as do men, and the rise in women's PACs that bundle money is likely a major reason.[27] Political activists and observers recognize the impact of women's PACs in soliciting contributions: "Ten years ago women were not writing checks." "Women have been notoriously un-educated about the need to get involved financially." "EMILY has loosened up a universe of donors that didn't give in the past."[28]

There are at least three reasons why women's PACs in general, and EMILY's List, The WISH List, and the Anthony List in particular, have been successful in mobilizing so many women to contribute so much money. First, some researchers find that feminist consciousness raises the level of women's political participation;[29] this would especially help explain the success of EMILY's List, by far the largest and wealthiest of the women's PACs. Second, other researchers have found that holding extreme views on either side of the abortion issue tends to increase individual participation levels, and that women's activism is even more likely than that of men to be driven by the abortion issue.[30] This would help explain the success of all three groups because all three use the abortion issue as a major litmus test for deciding which candidates to support. Third, women (but not men) tend to become more interested and engaged in politics when there are female candidates on the ballot and female incumbents in public office.[31] In this way, the success of the women's PACs has a cyclical effect: The more female candidates they help recruit and elect, the more women they can mobilize to contribute money; and the more money they collect, the more female candidates they can recruit and elect to public office.

Thus, we can go far in explaining the success of women's PACs in mobilizing contributors and raising money for female candidates. But until now, we have known very little about the political preferences and priorities, as well as the characteristics and activities, of the individuals who support these PACs with substantial contributions of funds. Of course, we are interested in the men who contribute as well: who they are, and why they are so committed to increasing the representation of women in politics. To find out more about them, we mailed surveys to people who contributed $200 or more to at least one of the three women's PACs, after obtaining their names and addresses from the FEC. In the chapters that follow, we examine in detail the women and men who help crack the political glass ceiling by contributing to EMILY's List, The WISH List, and the Anthony List.

OVERVIEW OF THIS BOOK

Having set the stage by describing the political and legal context in which these three women's PACs operate, we will provide more detailed information about EMILY's List, The WISH List, and the Anthony List in Chapter 2: how they were founded and by whom; how they have expanded in wealth, in size, and in scope; and how they fit into the evolving U.S. partisan alignment.

Chapter 3 presents information about the characteristics of donors to each PAC and how they are recruited, particularly through direct-mail appeals and personal networking. We find that these PACs receive their significant contributions mostly from well-heeled, highly educated activists, most of whom are women. Chapter 3 also compares the political activities and other group affiliations of contributors to each PAC. Contributors are similarly engaged in a wide array of electoral activities and organizations, with both overlapping and conflicting affiliations.

Chapter 4 compares the partisan and ideological affinities of contributors to each PAC. We find, for example, that contributors to the pro-choice Republican WISH List are both more moderate and more ambivalent in their partisan loyalties than are contributors to the pro-choice Democratic EMILY's List and the pro-life Anthony List. And while the three groups of donors share an interest in increasing the political representation of women, they are highly divergent in their attitudes toward, and commitment to, feminism. Chapter 4 also compares the political preferences and priorities of contributors to each PAC. The WISH List contributors tend to be the most moderate on most issues, but they are closer to those of EMILY's List on social issues such as gender roles, school prayer, gun control, and gay rights; they are closer to those of the Anthony List on such issues as social welfare, promotion of equality, the role of government, and national defense. And they are far to the right of both other groups in their support for the death penalty.

Chapter 5 compares the political preferences and priorities of the female contributors with those of the male contributors. There are, of course, far greater disparities among the donor groups than there are between the women and the men within each donor group. However, even within groups there is a tendency for the women to be less supportive than the men of the use of force. In addition, the women who contribute to EMILY's List profess even greater support than their male counterparts for feminism and gender equality.

Chapter 6 compares the political activities, attitudes, and priorities of the female contributors to the three PACS with women in general and with other female political contributors. We find the women's PAC contributors to be extremely active politically and especially polarized around issues related to feminism, compared to women in general and even to other female contributors. At the same time, contributors to all three women's PACS—even the socially conservative Anthony List—are much more supportive of women's equality in business, industry, and government than are women in general.

Finally, Chapter 7 presents the overall summary and conclusions, including assessments of the overriding ideological motivations to contribute serious money to women's PACs: liberal feminism for EMILY's List contributors, laissez-faire individualism for The WISH List contributors, and social conservatism for the Susan B. Anthony List contributors.

NOTES

1. "Rhetoric," Barbara Hinkson Craig and David M. O'Brien note, "has been a crucial element in the politics of abortion." The terms "pro-choice" and "pro-life," coined by activists on each side of the abortion debate, have become standard terms used in media and scholarly accounts of the politics of abortion. The use of these terms has become increasingly common with the passage of time, and are frequently used as well by the three organizations that are the focus of this book: EMILY's List and The WISH List frequently refer to themselves as pro-choice, and the Anthony List frequently refers to itself as pro-life, in organizational literature. We follow the convention by using these terms throughout the book. See Barbara Hinkson Craig and David M. O'Brien, *Abortion and American Politics* (Chatham, NJ: Chatham House, 1993), p. xv.
2. There is some controversy today over the actual views of Susan B. Anthony, and other feminists in the late nineteenth and early twentieth centuries, toward legalized abortion. The controversy revolves around who actually said what, since early articles were often unsigned or signed only with initials; the importance or unimportance of the abortion issue to early feminists; and the nature of the relationship between early feminists' statements about abortion and the modern debate between pro-life and pro-choice advocates. In the context of the earlier period, for example, the sexual double standard gave men much more sexual freedom than women, women were economically dependent on men and needed husbands to support them, and traditional sex roles within the patriarchal family as well as the larger society were not generally challenged, even by feminists, to anywhere near the extent that they are challenged today. In such a context, sexual freedom may have seemed liberating to men but oppressive to women, and the concept of a woman's control over her own body, often invoked by modern pro-choice advocates, had a different meaning than it does today. Many early feminists viewed sexual abstinence as the most realistic way to maintain autonomy and avoid victimization. For a fuller discussion of the issues surrounding the controversy, which is beyond the scope of this book, see Linda Gordon, "Voluntary Motherhood: The Beginnings of Feminist Birth Control Ideas in the United States," *Feminist Studies* 1, no. 3–4 (1978), pp. 5–22; Linda Gordon, *Woman's Body, Woman's Right: A Social History of Birth Control in America* (New York: Penguin Books, 1977); James C. Mohr, *Abortion in America: The Origins and Evolution of National Policy, 1800–1900* (New York: Oxford University Press, 1978); Dorothy McBride Stetson, *Women's Rights in the U.S.A.: Policy Debates and Gender Roles,* 2nd ed. (New York: Garland, 1997), Chapter 4; and Rachel MacNair, Mare Krane Derr, and Linda Naranjo-Huebl, eds., *Prolife Feminism Yesterday and Today* (New York: Sulzburger and Graham, 1995), the latter of which "attempts to document the continuum of feminist prolife thinking" (p. 1).
3. The Susan B. Anthony List is sometimes referred to as the Anthony List. When listed together, the three PACs will generally be listed in the order in which they were founded: EMILY's List in 1986, The WISH List in 1992, and the Anthony List in 1993.
4. Sidney Verba, Kay Lehman Schlozman, and Henry E. Brady, *Voice and Equality: Civic Voluntarism in American Politics* (Cambridge, MA: Harvard University Press, 1995), p. 255; Larry Makinson and the staff of the Center for Responsive Politics, *The Big Picture: The Money behind the 2000 Elections* (Washington, D.C.: Center for Responsive Politics, 2001); Peter Francia, John C. Green, Paul S. Herrnson, Lynda W. Powell, and Clyde Wilcox, *The Financiers of Congressional Elections: Investors, Ideologues, and Intimates* (New York: Columbia University Press, 2004).
5. For exceptions, see Clifford W. Brown, Jr., Lynda W. Powell, and Clyde Wilcox, *Serious Money: Fundraising and Contributing in Presidential Nomination Campaigns* (New York: Cambridge University Press, 1995); Francia, et al., *The Financiers of Congressional Elections;* Ruth Jones and Warren E. Miller, "Financing Campaigns: Macro Level Innovation and Micro Level Response," *Western Political Quarterly* 38 (1985), pp. 187–210; Benjamin A. Webster, Clyde Wilcox, Paul S. Herrnson, Peter L. Francia, John C. Green, and Lynda Powell, "Competing for Cash: The Individual Financiers of Congressional Elections," in *Playing Hardball: Campaigning for the U.S. Congress,* ed. Paul S. Herrnson (Upper Saddle River, NJ: Prentice Hall, 2001).
6. Information about the congresswomen comes from Philip D. Duncan and Brian Nutting, eds., *CQ's Politics in America 2000: The 106th Congress* (Washington, D.C.: Congressional Quarterly, Inc., 1999).

7. The limit on PAC contributions remains unchanged in the Bipartisan Campaign Reform Act (BCRA) of 2002, although further restrictions were placed on the electoral activities of interest groups, such as a ban on issue ads that mention candidates by name. Individual contributions were doubled from $1,000 to $2,000 in the BCRA, and an individual's overall contribution limit was raised in the BCRA to $95,000 from $25,000. For more information on campaign finance law and its implications and effects, see Frank J. Sorauf, *Inside Campaign Finance: Myths and Realities* (New Haven, CT: Yale University Press, 1992); Robert Biersack, Paul S. Herrnson, and Clyde Wilcox, eds., *Risky Business: PAC Decision-making in Congressional Elections* (Armonk, NY: M. E. Sharpe, 1994); John R. Wright, *Interest Groups and Congress: Lobbying, Contributions, and Influence* (Boston: Allyn & Bacon, 1996); Mark J. Rozell and Clyde Wilcox, *Interest Groups in American Campaigns* (Washington, D.C.: CQ Press, 1999); Paul S. Herrnson, *Congressional Elections: Campaigning at Home and in Washington,* 4th ed. (Washington, D.C.: CQ Press, 2004); Francia, et al., *The Financiers of Congressional Elections.*

8. Brown, Powell, and Wilcox, *Serious Money;* Rozell and Wilcox, *Interest Groups in American Campaigns;* Thomas R. Marshall, "Bundling the Cash: Why Do Interest Groups Bundle Donations?" *American Review of Politics* 18 (1997), pp. 291–308; Larry J. Sabato, *PAC Power: Inside the World of Political Action Committees* (New York: W. W. Norton, 1984); Sorauf, *Inside Campaign Finance.*

9. Barbara C. Burrell, *A Woman's Place is in the House: Campaigning for Congress in the Feminist Era* (Ann Arbor: University of Michigan Press, 1994); Kristin LaCour Dabelko and Paul S. Herrnson, "Women's and Men's Campaigns for the U.S. House of Representatives," *Political Research Quarterly* 50 (1997), pp. 121–135; Robert Darcy, Susan Welch, and Janet Clark, *Women, Elections, and Representation,* 2nd ed. (Lincoln, NE: University of Nebraska Press, 1994); Carole Jean Uhlaner and Kay Lehman Schlozman, "Candidate Gender and Congressional Campaign Receipts," *Journal of Politics* 48 (1986), pp. 30–50.

10. Susan J. Carroll, *Women as Candidates in American Politics,* 2nd ed. (Bloomington, IN: Indiana University Press, 1994); Dabelko and Herrnson, "Women's and Men's Campaigns for the U.S. House of Representatives"; Janet A. Flammang, *Women's Political Voice: How Women Are Transforming the Practice and Study of Politics* (Philadelphia, PA: Temple University Press, 1997); Candice J. Nelson, "Women's PACs in the Year of the Woman," in *The Year of the Woman: Myths and Realities,* ed. Elizabeth Adell Cook, Sue Thomas, and Clyde Wilcox (Boulder, CO: Westview Press, 1994); Jean Reith Schroedel and Nicola Mazumdar, "Into the Twenty-First Century: Will Women Break the Political Glass Ceiling?" in *Women and Elective Office: Past, Present, and Future,* ed. Sue Thomas and Clyde Wilcox (New York: Oxford University Press, 1998); Linda Witt, Karen M. Paget, and Glenna Matthews, *Running as a Woman: Gender and Power in American Politics* (New York: Free Press, 1994).

11. Nelson, "Women's PACs in the Year of the Woman"; Mark J. Rozell, "Helping Women Run and Win: Feminist Groups, Candidate Recruitment and Training," *Women and Politics* 21 (2000), pp. 101–116; Abigail McCarthy, "Women and Money and Politics: Can Susan and Emily Work Together?" *Commonweal* 124, no. 14 (1997), pp. 8–9.

12. See Eliza Newlin Carney, "Weighing In," *National Journal,* 13 June 1992, pp. 1399–1403; Burrell, *A Woman's Place is in the House;* Lisa Young, *Feminists and Party Politics* (Ann Arbor, MI: University of Michigan Press, 2000), pp. 203–205.

13. Dabelko and Herrnson, "Women's and Men's Campaigns for the U.S. House of Representatives"; Beth Donovan, "Women's Campaigns Fueled Mostly by Women's Checks," *Congressional Quarterly Weekly Report,* 17 October 1992, pp. 3269–3273; Witt, Paget, and Matthews, *Running as a Woman.*

14. Darcy, Welch, and Clark, *Women, Elections, and Representation;* Lee Ann Banaszak, "When Waves Collide: Cycles of Protest and the Swiss and American Women's Movements," *Political Research Quarterly* 49 (1996), pp. 839–860.

15. Flammang, *Women's Political Voice,* p. 189.

16. Center for the American Woman and Politics, Eagleton Institute of Politics, Rutgers University, *CAWP News and Notes* 10, no. 3 (1996); Susan L. Roberts, "Women's PACs: Evolution, Operation, and Outlook," presented at the annual meeting of the Southern Political Science Association, Atlanta, Georgia, 1992. See also Lisa Young, *Feminists and Party Politics,* pp. 41–42.

17. Peter L. Francia, "Early Fundraising by Nonincumbent Female Congressional Candidates: The Importance of Women's PACs," *Women and Politics* 23 (2001), pp. 7–20.

18. Jo Freeman, "Change and Continuity for Women at the Republican and Democratic National Conventions," *American Review of Politics* 18 (1997), pp. 353–368; Christina Wolbrecht, *The Politics of Women's Rights: Parties, Positions, and Change* (Princeton, NJ: Princeton University Press, 2000); Young, *Feminists and Party Politics*.
19. Rebecca Klatch, *Women of the New Right* (Philadelphia, PA: Temple University Press, 1987).
20. Nancy Burns, Kay Lehman Schlozman, and Sidney Verba, *The Private Roots of Public Action: Gender, Equality, and Political Participation* (Cambridge, MA: Harvard University Press, 2001); Verba, Schlozman, and Brady, *Voice and Equality*.
21. Larry Makinson and the staff of the Center for Responsive Politics, *The Big Picture* (see also their Web Site at www.opensecrets.org); Benjamin A. Webster, Clyde Wilcox, Paul S. Herrnson, Peter L. Francia, John C. Green, and Lynda Powell, "Competing for Cash: The Individual Financiers of Congressional Elections," in *Playing Hardball: Campaigning for the U.S. Congress*, ed. Paul S. Herrnson (Upper Saddle River, NJ: Prentice Hall, 2001); Francia, et al., *The Financiers of Congressional Elections*.
22. Flammang, *Women's Political Voice*; Burns, Schlozman, and Verba, *The Private Roots of Public Action*.
23. Burns, Schlozman, and Verba, *The Private Roots of Public Action*; Verba, Schlozman, and Brady, *Voice and Equality*.
24. M. Margaret Conway, Gertrude A. Steuernagel, and David W. Ahern, *Women and Political Participation: Cultural Change in the Political Arena* (Washington, D.C.: CQ Press, 1997); Verba, Schlozman, and Brady, *Voice and Equality*.
25. Flammang, *Women's Political Voice*.
26. Burns, Schlozman, and Verba, *The Private Roots of Public Action*; Verba, Schlozman, and Brady, *Voice and Equality*.
27. Webster, et al., "Competing for Cash."
28. Quoted in Beth Donovan, "Women's Campaigns Fueled Mostly by Women's Checks," *Congressional Quarterly Weekly Report*, 17 October 1992, p. 3270.
29. Conway, Steuernagel, and Ahern, *Women and Political Participation*; Flammang, *Women's Political Voice*.
30. Burns, Schlozman, and Verba, *The Private Roots of Public Action*; Verba, Schlozman, and Brady, *Voice and Equality*.
31. Burns, Schlozman, and Verba, *The Private Roots of Public Action*.

THE RISE OF WOMEN'S PACS

EMILY's List, The WISH List, and the Susan B. Anthony List are all women's political action committees, or PACs. They support female candidates; they are run mostly by women; and they receive most of their donations from women. All three PACs arose in the last few decades, mirroring the expansion of women's roles and opportunities in every aspect of electoral politics. All three have bundled contributions to candidates and engaged in other campaign support activities to great acclaim and success. All three share two major goals: electing more women and influencing abortion policy. But they differ in their partisanship, with EMILY's List supporting Democrats exclusively, The WISH List supporting Republicans exclusively, and the Susan B. Anthony List supporting candidates of both parties in theory, although the vast majority of their candidates are Republicans. The groups also diverge in their positions on the one political issue that determines which candidates they support: abortion. EMILY's List and The WISH List are pro-choice, and the Susan B. Anthony List is pro-life.

All three women's PACs emerged from the politics surrounding the second wave of the women's movement, which began in the mid-1960s and revolutionized gender relations and the role of women in society. Throughout the movement's first four decades, the number of women in male-dominated leadership positions and institutions throughout society has grown steadily. Politics is no exception, but here the growth has been especially slow. In the mid-1970s, a full decade into the women's movement, the percentages of women in Congress and in state legislatures still were stuck in the single digits. No woman won a state governorship without succeeding a husband until 1974. When EMILY's List was founded in 1985, women still held only 5 percent of congressional seats and barely 15 percent of state legislative seats and statewide offices. By 1993, the year that the Anthony List first emerged and one year after The WISH List was founded, women had gained 10 percent of congressional seats and just over 20 percent of state legislative and statewide offices.

While politics may still be "more exclusively limited to men than any other realm of endeavor,"[1] and gender parity in elective office remains elusive, the growth in female representation is on a slow but steady course. Women's PACs likewise continue to expand in number, size, and spending power. These two trends mutually affect each other. The growing participation of women in politics, as well as in other areas of power and influence, has opened the way for women's PACs and donor networks to gain public and financial support. In turn, support from women's PACs enhances the electoral success of women in politics.

This chapter discusses the rise and expansion of EMILY's List, The WISH List, and the Anthony List in the context of the second wave of the women's movement and the evolving partisan politics related to feminism and antifeminism.

PARTISAN POLITICS AND THE WOMEN'S MOVEMENT

Political parties today generally take opposing stands on feminist issues; feminists are prominent within the Democratic party coalition, while social conservatives favoring more traditional gender roles are prominent within the Republican party coalition.[2] But when the contemporary women's movement erupted in the 1960s, the Democratic and Republican parties were nearly indistinguishable in their stance toward women's rights. Both parties had claimed for decades to champion women's rights, yet neither party made it an active priority. If anything, the Republican party was slightly more supportive of gender equality, as groups of business and professional women active within the party advocated the removal of barriers to equal opportunities in employment and education. Their views, furthermore, were in line with laissez-faire conservative support for individualism and free markets. The Democratic party, meanwhile, still often took a protectionist stance toward women—favoring government regulations protecting women from long hours or harsh conditions in the workplace, for example—in keeping with labor union advocacy and party rhetoric about alleviating the plight of the poor and oppressed.

As the women's movement gained momentum in the late 1960s and early 1970s, and as the Civil Rights Act of 1964 largely invalidated protectionism in employment, the debate between protectionism and equality dissolved, and the major parties moved even closer to each other on women's rights and equality issues. The major issues identified with the movement, including abortion and sex discrimination, were cross-cutting issues, with no clear pattern of partisan support or opposition among voters or policymakers. In 1972, both parties promised similarly strong action favoring gender equality in their national platforms, and a bipartisan coalition in

Congress passed the Equal Rights Amendment (ERA), which would have enshrined gender equality in the U.S. Constitution if three-fourths of the state legislatures had gone on to ratify it. Further legislation promoting gender equality in areas ranging from salaries and consumer credit to education and employment flowed from Congress in the early 1970s.

In this bipartisan context, the first organizations to arise out of the second-wave women's movement also were bipartisan, eschewing affiliation with, or support for, either political party. This includes the first of the mass membership organizations and still the largest, the National Organization for Women (NOW), founded in 1967; it also includes the first group established with a principal focus on electoral politics, the National Women's Political Caucus (NWPC), founded in 1971. The first women's PAC, the Women's Campaign Fund, was established in 1974 by a bipartisan group of female activists, and it likewise supported women of both parties.

Soon, however, debates over women's rights issues began to evolve in a way that would come to polarize the parties. As the women's movement generated new opposition, an opposition revolving around support for traditional gender roles and anchored in conservative religious groups, women's issues were debated in terms of tradition versus liberation. The movement for women's liberation became associated with a more general rights agenda, African-American civil rights in particular, aligning it gradually with the Democratic party. In response to the rising influence of feminism in politics, many social conservatives of the religious right became politically mobilized in the 1970s by such organizations as Phyllis Schlafly's Stop ERA (which later became the Eagle Forum), the Moral Majority, and Concerned Women for America; they were followed by the Christian Coalition and the Family Research Council in the 1980s. All of them articulated opposition to many of the changes in gender and family relations that they associated with the women's movement. By the early 1980s these groups had aligned themselves with the Republican party. At the same time, laissez-faire conservatives and business interests, traditionally aligned with the Republican party, also began to distance themselves from the women's movement as feminist leaders called for more proactive government intervention to aid women and to fight sex discrimination. Thus, through a period of gradual issue evolution, the two parties were quite polarized around feminist issues by the early 1980s, and that polarization has increased over time into the twenty-first century.[3]

The abortion issue contributed to the polarization of party elites and voters by galvanizing opposition to the feminist movement, and energizing both sides, after the 1973 Supreme Court decision in *Roe v. Wade* struck down anti-abortion laws as violating the constitutional right to privacy. Although the abortion issue is separate from that of women's equality, and although views on women's rights and abortion rights are not perfectly aligned, the abortion issue has helped to shape and to sharpen the debate. Politically much more than a simple medical procedure, the legal right to an abortion from the mainstream feminist point of view symbolizes a break from traditional authority relationships, most particularly women's autonomy from the patriarchal family or patriarchal religious institutions. From the social conservative point of view, the legal right to an abortion also symbolizes a break—a break from family values and traditional or religious morality that help maintain order and security in the home and in the society at large. If the *Roe v. Wade* decision had not mobilized so many activists to join the drive to end legal abortion, sociologist Sara Diamond suggests, "the Christian Right would not have become a social movement formidable enough to swing elections."[4] Similarly, pro-choice activists stimulated a counterreaction that energized the broader women's rights movement and increased feminist organizational memberships, following *Roe v. Wade* and especially following two later cases in which the Supreme Court opened the door to further state restrictions on abortion, *Webster v. Reproductive Health Services* (1989) and *Planned Parenthood of Southeast Pennsylvania v. Casey* (1992).[5]

The abortion issue not only galvanized political activism on both sides, but it also contributed to partisan change, as the two major parties became increasingly polarized around the issue. At the time of the 1973 *Roe v. Wade* decision, abortion was still a cross-cutting issue, with no clear partisan lines of support. Over the following two decades, Democrats in Congress collectively became increasingly pro-choice while congressional Republicans voted increasingly pro-life. In 1980, the Republican party added rhetoric that was strongly pro-life to their presidential platform, and it dropped support for the ERA. Finally, voters themselves divided gradually along the same partisan lines in their attitudes toward abortion. The increasing partisan polarization on the abortion issue after the early 1970s conformed with the issue evolution model of partisan change, as mass public attitudes followed changes in elite rhetoric and behavior. By the 1990s, partisan polarization on the abortion issue reflected the same polarization as women's rights issues more generally.[6]

All this is not to say that pro-feminist and pro-choice attitudes are perfectly correlated, even in the contemporary U.S. context. Members of Feminists for Life, established in 1973, for example, consider legal abortion to be oppressive rather than liberating for women; it is, they say, another patriarchal form of violence and control over women. They further deny that the pro-life movement is uniformly part of the Christian Right; instead, many pro-life feminists view abortion as an ecumenical or secular human-rights issue.[7] These views have not made serious inroads into the Democratic party elite, however, especially among female Democratic activists and politicians. This is why the pro-life Anthony List, although officially bipartisan, has endorsed no more than a handful of Democratic candidates in its ten years of existence. This Democratic unity on the abortion issue helps to explain why the Democratic pro-choice EMILY's List is by far the largest and wealthiest of the women's PACs.

Republican elites, on the other hand, are more divided on the abortion issue, even though the official stance of the Republican party, as reflected in its presidential platforms since 1980, is pro-life. Conservative female activists, in particular, are split between two groups: (1) laissez-faire conservatives, who champion free-market policies and individual freedom, and who therefore tend to oppose governmental intervention into reproductive choices, including abortion; and (2) social conservatives, whose ties to traditional and religious moral views lead them to favor laws that prohibit abortion.[8] This breach among Republicans is both a blessing and a curse for the party. On the one hand, party leaders can claim big-tent party status, where people with opposing views can all find a home; on the other hand, intraparty conflict over the abortion issue saps energy, undermines unity, and exposes the party and its candidates to charges of inconsistency.

Both groups of conservative Republicans often criticize the contemporary women's movement. Laissez-faire conservatives feel that feminists rely excessively on the state in their support for various social welfare programs and active antidiscrimination policies. At the same time, many feel at least some affinity toward feminist demands for individual rights and equal opportunity regardless of sex. It is the social conservatives, generally affiliated with the religious right, who are most outspokenly antifeminist. Nevertheless, many Christian Right activists, particularly female leaders of such affiliated organizations as Concerned Women for America and Phyllis Schlafly's Eagle Forum, shape the debate over feminism in a way that promotes women's involvement in politics and other male-dominated domains while characterizing feminism as "selfish, antifamily, antireligious, and radical."[9] Especially in recent decades, social conservatives who promote traditional values and gender roles have realized that it is in their interest for women to become visibly involved in politics, including running for office, because it demonstrates the fact that not all female political elites are united around feminist goals and abortion rights.

As the two major parties have gradually polarized around feminist issues since the early 1970s, activists within the women's movement increasingly have embraced electoral politics as a major strategy for achieving their goals. The anti-establishment cast of the movement in its early years led activists initially to shun electoral politics. But feminist organizations that focused on recruiting, training, and electing women were up and running by the early 1970s. Today, electoral and partisan politics play an extraordinary role in the U.S. women's movement compared to women's movements in other countries.[10] It is in this context of partisan polarization around women's rights issues, and emphasis on electoral politics, that EMILY's List, The WISH List, and the Anthony List arose and flourished.

THE EMERGENCE OF EMILY's LIST, THE WISH LIST,
AND THE SUSAN B. ANTHONY LIST: 1980s–1990s

EMILY's List, The WISH List, and the Anthony List all were formed within a decade of each other, becoming both cause and consequence of a historical expansion in the number of women running for office and winning elections. All three organizations offer financial support by bundling individual contributions to their endorsed candidates as well as by making direct contributions. They also engage in a variety of other campaign activities, including the recruitment and training of candidates.[11]

EMILY's List was the first partisan women's PAC, entering the political scene as bipartisan cooperation on women's issues in general, and abortion in particular, was giving way to partisan polarization. It began in 1984 as an informal network of politically active friends including the current president, Ellen Malcolm, circulating lists and soliciting contributions for Democratic pro-choice female candidates; it became a formal PAC in 1986. The name EMILY, as explained in Chapter 1, stands for "Early Money Is Like Yeast" because "it makes the dough rise." The reference to rising "dough" refers to the importance of raising substantial amounts of money early in a campaign, especially for nonincumbents—either challengers or open-seat candidates—who have not already cultivated large fund-raising and support networks. Without early money, or "seed" money, it is difficult to demonstrate viability as a potential winner and to hire professional fund-raisers and other campaign consultants who can help increase the candidate's name recognition and credibility. Because so few women are incumbents and because incumbency is such a huge advantage in terms of fund-raising and name recognition, the founders of EMILY's List felt that incumbency was the biggest hurdle that female candidates faced, and early money could help them overcome the early obstacles. In addition to the incumbency factor, women are less likely than men to have the business and professional connections that can help with early fund-raising, and although the fund-raising aspect of candidacy is universally disliked, self-promotion is especially difficult for women.[12] Indeed, the seed money provided by women's PACs has had a significant impact on women's electoral success.[13] Thus, EMILY's List quickly became the model of success for many other PACs, with its contributions breaking the million-dollar mark in 1990 and climbing in every election since then. Since the early 1990s, EMILY's List has superseded all other women's PACs, and all but a handful of PACs in general, in total bundled and direct contributions—contributions that consistently reach into the several millions of dollars.

The WISH List (Women in the Senate and House) was founded in 1992 with the help and advice of EMILY's List leaders, adopting the financial networking and bundling techniques of the older PAC to support Republican pro-choice female candidates. Thus there was a substantial amount of cooperation among the two groups' leaders around the common goals of electing more women and promoting reproductive rights, despite their different partisan affiliations.[14] While never reaching the stratospheric heights of EMILY's List, The WISH List contributions have been in the hundreds of thousands of dollars in every election since their founding.

The Susan B. Anthony List was formed in 1993 in order to challenge the notion that female political elites are mostly pro-choice. A major impetus for its founding was the 1992 election, in which a record number of women were elected to Congress, state legislatures, and statewide office, prompting the media label "the Year of the Woman." None of the new female members of Congress, and only two women already in Congress, were pro-life.[15] Thus, in an effort to increase the percentage of women in public office who are pro-life, the Anthony List supports both pro-life female candidates, and candidates of either sex who run against pro-choice women. They employ a stringent definition of "pro-life" in selecting candidates; at the most, their candidates may support exceptions only for rape, incest, and saving the life of the mother in their opposition to legalized abortion. Most of their candidates are in fact women; in the last three elections, the percentage of women among the Anthony List's recommended candidates was 79 percent in 1998, 59 percent in 2000, and 72 percent in 2002.

Initially, the Anthony List, like EMILY's List and The WISH List, was strictly a PAC, with no affiliated lobbying arm or tax-deductible organization. Its fund-raising techniques were modeled largely after those of EMILY's List and The WISH List, including the bundling of individual contributions as well as direct contributions to recommended candidates, all of whom originally were women. In 1997, however, the PAC was replaced with a nonprofit 501(c)(4) educational and lobbying organization, also called the Susan B. Anthony List, and one year later, in 1998, a new affiliated PAC resumed collecting money to contribute to pro-life candidates, working to elect pro-life women and to defeat pro-choice women. Like EMILY's List and The WISH List, the Anthony List has enjoyed rapid growth in candidate contributions with every election.

MISSION, GOALS, AND STRATEGIES

Each of the three organizations has a mission to influence abortion policy, with a strategic focus on electoral politics. They emulate each other, and they oppose each other based on their partisanship and their views on the abortion issue. But even in this highly partisan era, when interparty conflict and even acrimony have reached historical heights, it is the abortion issue more than partisanship that divides them. This becomes clear when leaders of the three groups are asked in interviews about their organizational alliances and adversaries. The Anthony List executive director Jennifer Bingham cites pro-choice groups in general as the organization's major antagonists, including both EMILY's List and The WISH List specifically as well as a host of other pro-choice organizations such as NARAL Pro-Choice America and Planned Parenthood.[16] The WISH List's president, in turn, says the Anthony List is "not exactly our adversary, but our direct opposite."[17] There is greater affinity, on the other hand, between the two pro-choice groups. The WISH List president Pat Carpenter and EMILY's List president Ellen Malcolm say they do meet on occasion and provide some mutual emotional support, despite their different partisanship and despite their support on occasion for opposing candidates in the same election. "They're probably glad The WISH List exists,"[18] The WISH List's president says of EMILY's List. "They're like our cousins," EMILY's List's president says of The WISH List, "but not the Susan B. Anthony List."[19]

At the same time, there is some tension between the two pro-choice groups and their definitions of "pro-choice." Both state that their primary criterion for choosing to support candidates, apart from their partisanship, is that the candidates support the *Roe v. Wade* decision. But candidates supported by The WISH List may support some secondary restrictions on abortion or oppose funding for abortion in some cases, for example, without losing the organization's support. "Primarily, it's about whether abortion is safe and legal," says their president.[20] EMILY's List maintains a more stringent definition of "pro-choice" in selecting candidates, as well as a broader interpretation of abortion rights protected by *Roe v. Wade.* For example, EMILY's List withdrew support for one Democratic incumbent U.S. Senator, Mary Landrieu of Louisiana, despite the fact that she drew strong Republican opposition in the 2002 election, because of Landrieu's vote on a bill banning certain "late-term" abortion procedures that actually included some early-term procedures and that did not permit exceptions to protect the mother's health. The bill's supporters, says EMILY's List's president, "are wrong if they think it's not a violation of *Roe.*"[21]

While the abortion issue underlies the fundamental conflict among the three women's PACs, interpartisan conflict is also evident, especially in EMILY's List's own litany of major allies and adversaries. The most important allies cited by EMILY's List are the state and national Democratic party organizations, as well as "any group that's strong in the Democratic coalition in a given state," such as labor unions or environmentalists. The major adversaries cited are "Republicans" and "any big, wealthy Republican group," including the pharmaceutical industry, the insurance industry, the National Rifle Association, and the Club for Growth, a group that bundles contributions to Republican candidates.[22] This is in keeping with research demonstrating that "women's political groups affiliated with the Democratic Party have a much closer relationship with their party than do organizations that endorse Republican women."[23]

The WISH List and the Anthony List are allied somewhat more tenuously with the Republican party, and philosophical differences between the two PACs extend beyond the abortion issue. The WISH List's publicity materials—

its brochures and Web Site—emphasize a broad, laissez-faire conservative ideology that includes advocacy of limited government, individual freedoms and responsibility, and a strong national defense. The Anthony List's publicity materials are more narrowly focused on opposing abortion. Although the Republican party's official position on abortion is pro-life, it is the pro-choice WISH List that professes a closer working relationship with such party organizations as the Republican congressional campaign committees and the Republican Governors' Association. In fact, all of the major allies enumerated by the president of The WISH List are overtly Republican organizations that generally are considered to be among the more moderately conservative groups, such as the Republican Pro-Choice Coalition, the Republican Leadership Council, the Main Street Partnership, the Log Cabin Republicans, and the Ripon Society. Major adversaries cited are also key coalition partners within the Republican party, but they are in the socially conservative or religious right, including National Right to Life, Concerned Women for America, and the Family Research Council. These same WISH List antagonists are among the groups cited by the Anthony List as major allies.

In sum, the ties binding EMILY's List to the Democratic party are strong, as are the ties between The WISH List and the moderate or libertarian wing of the Republican party, yet both groups occasionally reach across party lines to provide mutual support. The Anthony List is the least overtly partisan PAC of the three, yet its ties to the religious right of the Republican party, as well as its stridently pro-life stance, seem to preclude any possibility of affinity or cooperation with the Republican WISH List, to say nothing of Democratic and pro-choice EMILY's List.

All three of these women's PACs are dedicated to helping women get elected to heavily male-dominated public institutions. Are they, then, feminist organizations? As this question is put to all three organization leaders, the president of EMILY's List is not surprisingly the only one to reply with a definitive "yes."[24] But neither The WISH List president nor the Anthony List executive director seems prepared to disavow feminism completely. The WISH List president does not hesitate to say that she herself is a feminist, stating, "[T]o me it's not a bad thing; the movement has done very positive things for women." Certainly, electing more women to public office is a feminist goal. Yet she notes that "to some people, this is a turnoff; to others, it's positive," and reactions often vary with individuals' own perception or definition of what feminism means.[25] The executive director of the Anthony List demurs even more: The Anthony List is "not necessarily" a feminist organization. But, "she notes: [W]e have a lot of members who are feminist," and "Susan B. Anthony was a feminist"; furthermore, the organization Feminists for Life helped to organize the Anthony List in the beginning. "Our main goal," she states, "is to make a better society for women and for children."[26]

EMILY's List, The WISH List, and the Anthony List represent the partisan and ideological diversity of women's PACs, and judging by their success in attracting members and donors, each represents a sizable bloc of activists. By the end of the 2002 electoral cycle, all three had more members than ever before: around 73,000 in EMILY's List, 4,000 in The WISH List, and 95,000 in the Anthony List. Membership is counted somewhat differently in the Anthony List than in the other two due to the difference in structure. A five-dollar minimum donation buys membership into the Anthony List; members are then asked to contribute to the Susan B. Anthony List Candidate Fund (the PAC) and to its recommended candidates, although it is not a requirement.[27] Members of EMILY's List and The WISH List pay $100 to join the PAC, and then they are asked to contribute at least $100 to each of two or more candidates recommended by the organization every election cycle (although in reality each organization will accept less money, and there are different levels of membership).

All three PACs collect the contributions made by their members to their recommended candidates and then forward those contributions to the candidates, a process known as "bundling," as explained in Chapter 1. The bundled contributions are legally reported to the Federal Election Commission—and then reported to the public by the FEC—as individual contributions, not PAC contributions. But politically, their effects are similar to those of PAC contributions because candidates know which organization the contributions come from. Bundling becomes, in many cases, a way for conduit PACs to raise citizen interest and awareness, maximize their strength, and contribute more to a given candidate than the legal limit of $5,000 per election. From the perspective of the individual donor, bundling both helps her decide which candidates to support and sends a political message along with the money; in the case of these three PACs, that message is about abortion policy. EMILY's List, The WISH List, and the Anthony List all contribute money to candidates directly as well, but most of their contributions to candidates have always been through bundling.

Bundling was pioneered by the environmental group Council for a Livable World in the 1960s, even before campaign finance reforms of the 1970s imposed limits on group and individual contributions, and it is widely used by groups across the ideological spectrum.[28] But it was EMILY's List that brought the bundling technique to widespread public attention with its enormous total contribution amounts, which made it a "media phenomenon" by the early 1990s.[29] In the 1995–1996 election cycle, for example, EMILY's List bundled more money to candidates than any other conduit PAC; The WISH List, which had begun bundling just two electoral cycles previously with advice from EMILY's List leaders, was seventh on the list.[30] EMILY's List's total contributions to candidates remain consistently at or near the top of all PACs. Further, PACs that focus on the abortion issue rank among the top-ten types of single-issue and ideological PACs in candidate contributions, thanks in no small part to EMILY's List, The WISH List, and the Anthony List.[31]

Internally, the process of deciding which candidates to support in each election cycle is similar in all three PACs, with the main exception related to the sheer size of EMILY's List. EMILY's List employs a staff of about fifty people in its Washington, D.C., and San Francisco offices handling various organizational functions, including research on the candidates for review by group leaders. The candidate research at The WISH List and the Anthony List is handled largely by the executive directors, each of whom has a staff of about five people. All three groups have a committee or board that makes the final decision on candidate endorsement. Aside from the differences in partisanship and views on abortion, all three groups look for similar traits in recruiting and endorsing candidates: They should be articulate, and they should be viable as candidates. Viability may include a record of community service or local political experience that would generate some name recognition, and generally it must include a network of supporters, access to campaign money, and some campaign organization already in place. As the three groups have grown, they have branched out into areas of training and recruitment in order to increase the number of potentially viable female candidates. Thus, although candidate viability automatically increases with an endorsement by any of these groups—"We've become the political equivalent of the 'Good Housekeeping Seal of Approval,'" notes EMILY's List[32]—the most desirable candidates are not those starting from scratch.

In addition, all three groups are always on the lookout for open seats—and for vulnerable incumbents as well, although the latter are more rare. Incumbents in U.S. politics are especially difficult to beat because they have developed sizable support networks and financial reserves, reinforced by continual support from PACs and individuals who know that incumbents seldom lose. Thus, backing a challenger to an incumbent is usually a futile enterprise, unless the incumbent is particularly vulnerable due to scandal, partisan misfortune, or changes in the nature of the district. That is why EMILY's List asserts: "Contrary to conventional wisdom, the biggest barrier to electing women is not gender—it's the power of incumbency."[33] Consequently, the best bet for expanding the number of women in elective office is to back candidates in open-seat races, where there is no incumbent running. It also is important, however, to find quality candidates to challenge vulnerable incumbents—and to protect the female incumbents already in office.

Not all PACs follow the same strategy in deciding whom to support, however. The most incumbent-friendly PACs are those that follow the "access" strategy: contributing mostly to sure winners, especially those in key leadership positions or on key committees, regardless of the candidates' partisanship. The PACs of many corporations and trade associations, for example, may follow this strategy in order to gain access to key lawmakers on low-visibility legislation that could affect their particular business or industry. Ideological and single-issue PACs such as EMILY's List, The WISH List, and the Anthony List, on the other hand, more often favor "ideological" strategies, in which they are more concerned with supporting candidates with particular views than cultivating ties to incumbents of either party. Such groups are more likely to support challengers and especially open-seat candidates, knowing that an incumbent who already does not agree with the group ideologically or on key high-salience issues such as abortion are not likely to be swayed to change their votes through lobbying efforts.[34]

As the number of female incumbents has grown at every level of government, each of the three women's PACs has more incumbents who fit their criteria for receiving contributions. At the same time, strategic ideological PACs do not want to spend limited resources on incumbents who are sure winners, when there are potentially viable challengers and open-seat candidates in other races who need financial assistance. Thus, decision making involves determining which favored incumbents are vulnerable and need money, which opposition incumbents are sufficiently vulnerable to warrant supporting their challengers, and which open-seat candidates are the best bets in terms of both viability and suitability from the PAC's point of view.

Leaders of EMILY's List are the most adamant about not supporting incumbents, unless they draw serious opposition, in order to reserve resources mostly for open-seat candidates.[35] Indeed, of the thirty-nine federal and gubernatorial candidates who received bundled or direct contributions from EMILY's List in 2002, only 23 percent were incumbents, while half were open-seat candidates and the other 28 percent were challengers. Leaders of both EMILY's List and the Anthony List state that the proportion of incumbents they support in each election cycle has not increased over time. Just one-third of the Anthony List's thirty-two endorsed candidates in 2002 were incumbents, while nearly half (44 percent) were open-seat candidates and 22 percent were challengers.[36] The WISH List supported incumbents the most: Half of over 200 candidates endorsed in the 2002 electoral cycle were incumbents, compared to 26 percent open-seat candidates and 22 percent challengers.[37] The WISH List endorsed so many more candidates than the others because of a recent change in operations, a change that both of the other women's PACs are also beginning to make: They are focusing increasingly on state- and local-level politics rather than concentrating exclusively on congressional and gubernatorial candidates. This is just one area in which EMILY's List, The WISH List, and the Anthony List are all expanding as their resources grow.

GROWTH AND EXPANSION: INTO THE TWENTY-FIRST CENTURY

In addition to their steady growth in both resources and membership over the years, EMILY's List, The WISH List, and the Anthony List have expanded their operations to include such functions as training, voter drives, and other forms of campaign support. They also have branched out from the federal to the state and local levels in their candidate support and other political activities.

EMILY's List spent the first four election cycles of its existence raising money and contributing to candidates, having evolved from a group of friends gathering donations to a nationally renowned conduit PAC. Then in 1994 it added more services, including the training of both candidates and campaign staff as well as campaign-related research. It also piloted a voter mobilization program called "Women Vote!," working with state Democratic parties to identify and contact voters, monitor public opinion through surveys and focus groups, and conduct issue advocacy campaigns. By 2002 the Women Vote! project was operating in 28 states. EMILY's List's new Campaign Corps program trains recent college graduates as campaign staff, placing them with its chosen candidates' campaigns. The WISH List, too, added candidate identification, recruitment, and training activities to its financial support network. The Anthony List, since regrouping as a political and educational membership organization with a connected PAC in 1997, supports its candidates and the pro-life cause with a variety of activities beyond fund-raising, including training programs for candidates and grassroots activists, public information campaigns, voter drives, lobbying, and issue advocacy.

Growth and expansion require money—and all three PACs had more money than ever in the 2002 election cycle, despite what EMILY's List euphemistically calls a "challenging fund-raising environment."[38] First, 2002 was a midterm election, when voters and contributors tend to be less interested and energized than in presidential election years. Second, the economy had slumped in 2001–2002, leaving people generally with less money to give. And third, the terrorist attacks of September 11, 2001, had a negative impact on political fund-raising and participation nationwide. Despite these challenges, all three organizations raised and contributed record amounts of money in 2002, mostly through bundling.

EMILY's List contributed a total of $9.7 million dollars to candidates in 2002, bundling $9.1 million to 27 recommended congressional and gubernatorial candidates, and directly contributing another half million dollars to 246 candidates at the state and national levels. It spent an additional $8.7 million on the Women Vote! program, and over $3 million on campaign services such as training and research.[39]

The WISH List contributed a total of $767,000 to more than 200 candidates at the national, state, and local levels, bundling just over $400,000 of that amount and contributing the rest to candidates directly.[40]

The Anthony List's PAC contributions totaled to just under $500,000, nearly $300,000 of which was bundled individual contributions. In addition, the PAC spent another $125,000 on independent expenditures to help their chosen candidates' campaigns with advertisements and voter drives. The Anthony List parent organization raised another $3.6 million for its lobbying and educational activities.[41]

Each one of the three PACs, then, reports that it bundled substantially larger amounts of money to candidates than it contributed directly. Yet even those figures may underestimate the amount of money received by candidates as a result of the political activities of EMILY's List, The WISH List, and the Anthony List. Because each PAC presents its members with information about candidates, including their positions on a variety of issues in addition to abortion, members may use that information in deciding to contribute directly to candidates rather than send the contributions by way of the PAC. "I use the recommendations and the great information sheets that they put together on the candidates and the races to guide my donations," one EMILY's List contributor writes on his survey questionnaire; "I usually support the candidates directly rather than through EMILY's List."

Perhaps the biggest change in all three organizations is their newly increased focus on state-level politics and support for candidates at the state and local levels. All three began by supporting federal candidates as well as a few candidates for statewide office, especially for state governor. But they began the twenty-first century with a new emphasis on cultivating more support, more grassroots activity, and more female candidate recruitment at the lower levels, particularly for state legislatures. There are two major reasons for this new attention to politics below the federal level. First, many candidates earn the experience and credibility to run for national office by first running and serving at the state and local levels; thus, recruiting at the lower levels can build a "farm team" for national politics.[42] Second, state governments have authority over broad areas of policy independently of the national government, and the trend in recent decades has been for Congress and the courts to grant the states even more authority over health care, welfare, and other policies. States would certainly have the power to restrict or even criminalize abortion if a future and more conservative U.S. Supreme Court overturned *Roe v. Wade*.[43]

The three PACs thus have a stake in expanding their involvement in the states. The WISH List led the way in 2000 by extending its campaign services—from raising and bundling contributions to recruiting candidates—to the state and local levels, especially for state legislative candidates. EMILY's List began training and contributing directly to state legislative candidates in 2002, and it plans to devote increasing amounts of resources and energy to state and local politics in future elections. The Anthony List, while not yet contributing to candidates below the statewide level, has increased its campaign staff and grassroots training efforts in various states, in conjunction with other pro-life groups. In sum, all three women's PACs are not only larger, but they also are more diversified, in the complex political environment of the early twenty-first century.

CONCLUSION

EMILY's List, The WISH List, and the Anthony List were founded between 1986 and 1993, at a time when the women's movement, and the organizations that arose both in support and in reaction to the movement, had become strongly oriented toward electoral politics. It was also a time of increasing partisan polarization around feminist issues generally, and the abortion issue in particular. EMILY's List, the first partisan women's PAC, quickly became one of the largest and most lucrative donor networks in the entire PAC universe. The pro-choice Democratic EMILY's List, the pro-choice Republican WISH List, and the pro-life Anthony List all have grown with every election, increasing their membership base and their contribution amounts, and expanding their array of services to candidates and their campaigns. The groups also have branched out into state and local politics, with plans to increase their involvement at the state level while maintaining their prominent role in national politics.

In the chapters that follow, we examine the characteristics, activities, and attitudes of these PACs' major contributors, based on the survey of persons who contributed $200 or more to EMILY's List, The WISH List, or the Anthony List.

NOTES

1. Wendy Brown, *Manhood and Politics: A Feminist Reading in Political Theory* (Totowa, NJ: Rowman and Littlefield, 1988), p. 4.
2. The following discussion on the evolution of the political parties vis-à-vis women's rights draws from Jo Freeman, "Whom You Know Versus Whom You Represent: Feminist Influence in the Democratic and Republican Parties," in *The Women's Movements of the United States and Western Europe: Consciousness, Political Opportunity, and Public Policy*, ed. Mary Fainsod Katzenstein and Carol M. Mueller (Philadelphia, PA: Temple University Press, 1987); Jo Freeman, "Change and Continuity for Women at the Republican and Democratic National Conventions," *American Review of Politics* 18 (1997), pp. 353–368; Christina Wolbrecht, *The Politics of Women's Rights: Parties, Positions, and Change* (Princeton, NJ: Princeton University Press, 2000); and Lisa Young, *Feminists and Party Politics* (Ann Arbor, MI: University of Michigan Press, 2000).
3. Wolbrecht, *The Politics of Women's Rights*; Sara Diamond, *Not by Politics Alone: The Enduring Influence of the Christian Right* (New York: Guilford Press, 1998).
4. Diamond, *Not by Politics Alone*, p. 132; see also Kristin Luker, *Abortion and the Politics of Motherhood* (Berkeley, CA: University of California Press, 1984); Rebecca E. Klatch, *Women of the New Right* (Philadelphia, PA: Temple University Press, 1987).
5. Wolbrecht, *The Politics of Women's Rights*, pp. 124–125, 158; Anne N. Costain, *Inviting Women's Rebellion: A Political Process Interpretation of the Women's Movement* (Baltimore, MD: Johns Hopkins University Press, 1992); Jane J. Mansbridge, *Why We Lost the ERA* (Chicago: University of Chicago Press, 1986); Nancy E. McGlen and Karen O'Connor, *Women, Politics, and the American Society* (Englewood Cliffs, NJ: Prentice Hall, 1995).
6. Greg D. Adams, "Abortion: Evidence of an Issue Evolution," *American Journal of Political Science* 41 (1997), pp. 718–737. See also Young, *Feminists and Party Politics*; Barbara Hinkson Craig and David M. O'Brien, *Abortion and American Politics* (Chatham, NJ: Chatham House, 1993).
7. Rachel MacNair, Mare Krane Derr, and Linda Naranjo-Huebl, eds., *Prolife Feminism Yesterday and Today* (New York: Sulzberger and Graham, 1995).
8. Klatch, *Women of the New Right*.
9. Wolbrecht, *The Politics of Women's Rights*, p. 173; see also Diamond, *Not by Politics Alone*, p. 127; Klatch, *Women of the New Right*.
10. Young, *Feminists and Party Politics*; Linda Witt, Karen M. Paget, and Glenna Matthews, *Running as a Woman: Gender and Power in American Politics* (New York: Free Press, 1994); Mark J. Rozell, "Helping Women Run and Win: Feminist Groups, Candidate Recruitment and Training," *Women and Politics* 21 (2000), pp. 101–116.

11. Information about the three organizations, unless cited otherwise, comes from author interviews with the following organization leaders, conducted between June 2 and June 10, 2003: Jennifer Bingham, Executive Director, the Susan B. Anthony List; Pat Giardina Carpenter, President, The WISH List; Ellen R. Malcolm, President and Co-Founder, and Sheila O'Connell, Senior Advisor, EMILY's List. See also each organization's Web Site: EMILY's List: http://www.emilyslist.org; The WISH List: http://www.thewishlist.org; the Susan B. Anthony List: http://www.sba-list.org.

12. Witt, Paget, and Matthews, *Running as a Woman*.

13. Peter L. Francia, "Early Fundraising by Nonincumbent Female Congressional Candidates: The Importance of Women's PACs," *Women and Politics* 23 (2001), pp. 7–20.

14. Barbara C. Burrell, *A Woman's Place is in the House: Campaigning for Congress in the Feminist Era* (Ann Arbor, MI: University of Michigan Press, 1994); Susan J. Carroll, *Women as Candidates in American Politics*, 2nd ed. (Bloomington, IN: University of Indiana Press, 1994); Craig A. Rimmerman, "New Kids on the Block: The WISH List and the Gay and Lesbian Victory Fund in the 1992 Elections," in *Risky Business? PAC Decisionmaking in Congressional Elections*, ed. Robert Biersack, Paul S. Herrnson, and Clyde Wilcox (Armonk, NY: M. E. Sharpe, 1994); Mark J. Rozell, "WISH List: Pro-Choice Women in the Republican Congress," in *After the Revolution: PACs, Lobbies, and the Republican Congress*, ed. Robert Biersack, Paul S. Herrnson, and Clyde Wilcox (Boston: Allyn and Bacon, 1999); Frank J. Sorauf, *Inside Campaign Finance: Myths and Realities* (New Haven, CT: Yale University Press, 1992).

15. The Susan B. Anthony List Web Site, www.sba-list.org (accessed March 31, 2003).

16. Interview with Jennifer Bingham, Executive Director, the Susan B. Anthony List, June 6, 2003.

17. Interview with Pat Giardina Carpenter, President, The WISH List, June 3, 2003.

18. Ibid.

19. Interview with Ellen R. Malcolm, President, and Sheila O'Connell, Senior Advisor, EMILY's List, June 5, 2003.

20. Carpenter interview. See also Rozell, "WISH List: Pro-Choice Women in the Republican Congress."

21. Malcolm and O'Connell interview.

22. Ibid.

23. Rosalyn Cooperman, "Party Organizations and the Recruitment of Women Candidates to the U.S. House since the 'Year of the Woman,'" presented at the annual meeting of the American Political Science Association, San Francisco, 2001, p. 16.

24. Malcolm interview.

25. Carpenter interview.

26. Bingham interview.

27. A notice on the Susan B. Anthony List Web Site states: "Your contribution to the Susan B. Anthony List automatically activates (or renews) your membership with the Susan B. Anthony List." See http://www.catholic.org/sba/generic_contribute.php (accessed August 2, 2003).

28. Thomas R. Marshall, "Bundling the Cash: Why Do Interest Groups Bundle Donations?" *American Review of Politics* 18 (1997), pp. 291–308; Richard H. Mayberry, Jr., and Kristine E. Heine, "PAC Counsel: Bundling Makes Strange Bedfellows," *Campaigns and Elections* (July–August, 1986), pp. 76–78; Larry J. Sabato, *PAC Power: Inside the World of Political Action Committees* (New York: W. W. Norton, 1990); Frank J. Sorauf, *Inside Campaign Finance.*

29. Burrell, *A Woman's Place is in the House*, p. 124.

30. Marshall, "Bundling the Cash," p. 293.

31. Larry Makinson and the staff of the Center for Responsive Politics, *The Big Picture: The Money Behind the 2000 Elections* (Washington, D.C.: The Center for Responsive Politics, 2001), p. 74–75. Other single-issue and ideological types in the top ten include general conservative/Republican PACs, general liberal/Democratic PACs, and PACs that focus on foreign policy, women's issues, human rights, environmental policy, and gun policy.

32. *Notes From Emily*, March 2003, p. 2.

33. Ibid.

34. For more on PAC strategy and decision making, see Sorauf, *Inside Campaign Finance;* Richard Hall and Frank Wayman, "Buying Time: Moneyed Interests and the Mobilization of Bias in Congressional Committees," *American Political Science Review* 84 (1990), pp. 417–438;

Paul S. Herrnson, *Congressional Elections: Campaigning at Home and in Washington*, 4th ed. (Washington, D.C.: CQ Press, 2004), Chapter 5.
35. Malcolm and O'Connell interview.
36. Bingham interview.
37. Carpenter interview.
38. Malcolm and O'Connell interview.
39. Ibid; *Notes from Emily*, March, 2003, pp. 4–6.
40. Carpenter interview.
41. Bingham interview.
42. Carpenter interview.
43. *Notes from Emily*, March, 2003, p. 3.

ATTRIBUTES AND ACTIVITIES
OF THE MAJOR CONTRIBUTORS

Large donors make a large difference. Congress recognized the importance of large contributions in the electoral process when it passed the
Federal Election Campaign Act (FECA) in 1971. One of the major provi-
sions of FECA was public disclosure: The names of all individuals who contributed $200 or more to a candidate or contributed $200 or more to a PAC
would now be available to the public. Such disclosure has been a boon to
political scientists and other observers who are interested in who gives how
much to whom.

The major contributors to EMILY's List, The WISH List, and the Susan
B. Anthony List Candidate Fund represent only a small percentage of the
total memberships, but they provide a major portion of the PACs' bud-
gets. In the 2002 election cycle, just 9 percent of EMILY's List's members
contributed $200 or more to the organization, but those contributions to-
taled over a third of the PAC's total receipts. Sixteen percent of The WISH
List's members contributed $200 or more to the group, but their total do-
nations made up 44 percent of the PAC's receipts. Fewer than 1 percent of
the members of the Susan B. Anthony List gave $200 or more to the group's
affiliated PAC, representing 30 percent of the PAC's overall receipts for
that cycle.[1]

All of these contributors presumably share an interest in abortion policy and also share an interest in electing more women with compatible
views. But what else do the contributors to these groups have in common,
and how great are their differences? How much of a priority is the abortion issue relative to the other issues in their political world? Given their
interest in increasing women's representation, what are their feelings about
feminism more broadly? These are some of the questions that we explore
using our Survey of Women's PAC Contributors. In this chapter, we take
a look first at the general social characteristics and political activities of
the contributors.[2]

THE SURVEY OF WOMEN'S PAC CONTRIBUTORS

The population surveyed consists of persons who contributed $200 or more to EMILY's List, to The WISH List, or to the Anthony List. Their names and addresses were obtained from the Federal Election Commission, the independent federal agency established by FECA to enforce campaign finance laws and to make campaign contribution information publicly accessible. The data come from four different surveys conducted between 1998 and 2000. The first survey was mailed in 1998 to the entire population of persons who contributed $200 or more to The WISH List and to a numerically matched sample of the much larger group who contributed at least $200 to EMILY's List, both during the 1996 election cycle. Respondents in both groups are overwhelmingly women, as are the full populations of contributors to these PACs. To expand the number of men in the analysis, a second survey was mailed in 1999 to all of the men in the 1996 EMILY's List database. A third survey was mailed in 2000 to the entire population of persons who contributed at least $200 to the Anthony List during the 1998 election cycle. There is almost no overlap of contributors among the three organizations; only three respondents contributed to both EMILY's List and The WISH List, and none of the Anthony List respondents had contributed to the other two.

Our aim was to reach as diverse a set of women's PAC contributors as possible, in terms of both partisanship and ideology, by targeting a Democratic pro-choice PAC (EMILY's List), a Republican pro-choice PAC (The WISH List), and a pro-life PAC (the Anthony List).[3] Appendix A describes the survey in more detail. Appendix B reproduces the questions asked in the three surveys, all of which are identical except for the words "EMILY's," "WISH," and "Susan B. Anthony," which correspond to the respondent's organization, and except for a question about vote choice in the 2000 presidential election, which was added to the later Susan B. Anthony List questionnaire.

SOCIOECONOMIC CHARACTERISTICS

Political contributors in the $200-and-over range are generally quite affluent, well educated, and disproportionately white and male.[4] Those who contribute to the three women's PACs also are affluent, highly educated, and disproportionately white—but they are mostly women, not men. EMILY's List and The WISH List major contributors are overwhelmingly women—94 percent and 90 percent respectively—as are more than half (54 percent) of the major contributors to the Anthony List. But among major contributors to congressional and presidential candidates generally, fewer than a quarter are women.[5] Thus, while major contributors to the three women's PACs are linked to major contributors generally by their high socioeconomic status, their gender balance sets them apart.

Fully 87 percent of the women's PAC contributors have household incomes exceeding $80,000, ranging from 79 percent for the Anthony List and 87 percent for EMILY's List to 95 percent for The WISH List, compared to 18 percent of the general public in 1998.[6] Their education level is astonishing; nearly all (93 percent) have college degrees and most have graduate or professional degrees, ranging from 47 percent for The WISH List and 51 percent for the Anthony List to 66 percent for EMILY's List contributors. In comparison, only a quarter of the general public had graduated from college in 1998, and 8 percent had graduate or professional degrees.[7] Most contributors are married: two-thirds of The WISH List and EMILY's List donors and three-fourths of the Anthony List donors. Nearly all are white—fewer than 1 percent describe themselves as African American, Asian American, American Indian, or Latino—and each group's median age is in the fifties—fifty for the Anthony List, fifty-five for The WISH List, and fifty-eight for EMILY's List.

Consistent with their high socioeconomic status, most contributors to the three women's PACs are employed outside the home, primarily in high-status professional or managerial occupations; retirees (one-fifth of The WISH List and Anthony List donors, and 29 percent of EMILY's List donors) were similarly employed. At least 80 percent of contributors to each women's PAC are employed in managerial or professional specialty fields, compared to only 30 percent of the general public.[8] However, there are some telling differences in career choice among the three groups. The WISH List donors are much more likely to hold managerial positions in business or finance (56 percent as opposed to 23 percent for EMILY's List and 31 percent for the Anthony List), not surprising since The WISH List donors most often fit the laissez-faire conservative mold favoring minimal government intervention in the free market. EMILY's List contributors are twice as likely as the others to work as teachers (16 percent) and ten times more likely to work as physicians (10 percent) compared to the other two groups. At least 11 percent of each donor group works in the legal profession, but Anthony List donors are nearly twice as likely to be attorneys (20 percent). Anthony List contributors also are much more likely to list their occupation as homemaker—11 percent, compared to only 1 percent of the other two groups.

Greater still are the differences in religious affiliation and religiosity among the three women's PACs. The WISH List contributors are the most Protestant of the three groups (66 percent, compared to 40 percent for each of the other two), while Anthony List contributors are by far the most Roman Catholic (56 percent compared to fewer than 6 percent for each of the other two). Among Protestants, two-thirds of the Anthony List donors, but fewer than 1 percent of the other two groups, describe themselves as evangelicals. EMILY's List contributors are the most likely to belong to the Jewish faith

(25 percent compared to 13 percent for The WISH List and 4 percent for the Anthony List). EMILY's List contributors also are the most likely to profess no religious preference (24 percent; 18 percent for The WISH List). All Anthony List donors claim some religious affiliation, and they are most likely to be religiously active; more than three-fourths of them attend religious services weekly, compared to fewer than 10 percent of each of the other two groups. Conversely, more than half of both EMILY's List and The WISH List donors, but only 6 percent of the Anthony List donors, attend religious services no more than a few times a year. Two-thirds of the Anthony List donors believe that "the Bible is God's word and all it says it true," in contrast to only 10 percent in The WISH List and 1 percent in EMILY's List. These differences in religiosity and fundamentalist Christian belief between the pro-life Anthony List donors and donors to the two pro-choice organizations are no surprise, given the frequent identification between conservative Christian groups and the pro-life cause.

In sum, the religious differences, and to some extent the career differences, among the major contributors to EMILY's List, The WISH List, and the Anthony List reflect their differences in partisanship and their positions on the abortion issue. But the three donor groups resemble each other, and they resemble major contributors in general, in their high socioeconomic status. In fact, contributing money is exceptional among political activities in that income, and it is by far the most important factor in determining who gives, and how much; it is the activity in which the economically disadvantaged are most underrepresented.[9] At the same time, the major contributors to the three women's PACs are predominantly female, which sets them apart from major political contributors more generally. Women, more than men, are driven to participate politically by their views on the abortion issue, whether pro-life or pro-choice, and women also become more interested and engaged in politics when women are on the ballot.[10] Thus, EMILY's List, The WISH List, and the Anthony List are in a good position to motivate participation among women. But, at least among their major donors—those in the $200-or-more range—they have not necessarily motivated new contributors so much as offered activists another channel for their political action. As we will see in the following section, the three PACs' major donors are active in a wide range of political pursuits.

POLITICAL TRUST, POLITICAL EFFICACY, AND POLITICAL ACTIVITY

Major contributors to EMILY's List, The WISH List, and the Anthony List share a high degree of political efficacy and activism. They are confident in their ability to influence government, and they channel that confidence into active political participation, contributing time and energy as well as money. Trust in government is another matter; here, the three donor groups diverge.

EMILY's List contributors are evenly split on whether or not, "generally speaking, the government in Washington can be trusted to do what is right." But two-thirds of The WISH List contributors and nearly all (98 percent) of the Anthony List contributors disagree that the government can be trusted.

The relatively greater trust in government among EMILY's List's contributors may reflect the Democrats' generally more favorable stance toward government intervention in domestic affairs. Still, only half of EMILY's List donors express such trust in government, and this comment from an EMILY's List respondent may represent the lack of trust expressed by the other half: "It is vital that we elect and maintain both a Democratic president and Congress. The federal courts have been transformed from an institution that was favorable to individual rights, most particularly those of women and minorities, to one that is very hostile to those same rights."[11] That is, EMILY's List supporters likely are divided between supporting strong government in such areas as social welfare and civil rights on the one hand, and fearing heavy-handedness from a government perceived as too conservative on the other hand. Comments from The WISH List contributors convey more of a laissez-faire distrust in government generally, for example: "I vote for women who have a strong sense of self and don't expect government to be the panacea for their life. I like self-reliance and I believe we as a nation expect the government to be able to control all social issues."

Why would contributors to the Anthony List be so overwhelmingly distrustful of government, given their preference for strongly enforced government laws prohibiting abortion? The following comments from Anthony List respondents demonstrate how some of them associate government with the feminist and liberal principles they oppose: "Women do not need government help to succeed. Feminists want women to believe they are victims. . . . [W]omen always will be influential, as long as we don't believe that we are inferior or need special help." "I think the majority are militant feminists, liberal, pro-abortion and believe in tax and spend policies, pro-government regulation, pro-big government." "Support womanhood. Support motherhood. Don't let radical antiwomen feminists, governments, control freaks like Planned Parenthood, the UN, and so on, take control of our ability to bring forth life."

Despite their differences in governmental trust, the major contributors to the three PACs share a belief in their ability to make a difference, and to influence policy by participating in the political process; they have a high degree of political efficacy. This seems obvious; why would they contribute substantial amounts of money if they felt it was being thrown to the wind? But it is interesting to observe the gulf between these contributors and the public in terms of their perceived ability to capture the government's attention. Large majorities of the women's PAC contributors—85 percent of EMILY's List, and 79 percent of both The WISH List and the Anthony List—disagree that "people like me don't have any say about what the government does." In contrast, only 39 percent of the voting-age public, represented by respondents to the 1996 National Election Study (commonly known as NES),[12] disagree with that statement. Conversely, 52 percent of the public, but only 15 percent of the women's PAC contributors, feel that people have no say. Similar majorities of all three groups of women's PAC contributors disagree with the statement: "I don't think public officials care much about what people like me think." Even larger majorities of the major contributors—more than 90 percent—feel they "have a pretty good understanding of the important issues facing this country." Such confidence among the contributors underlies a willingness to participate actively in politics.

The women's PAC contributors do participate in electoral politics, at rates far above those of the average citizen. All of them, of course, have made large contributions, and this alone sets them apart; only 12 percent of the general public reported making political contributions of any kind, and fewer than 1 percent of voting-age adults contribute to candidates in the $200-plus range.[13] But they are exceptionally active in other ways, too (see Table 3.1). More than three-fourths of them talk to other people about candidates or parties, compared to 29 percent of the general public. Well over half of the women's PAC contributors on average show support by displaying a campaign button, bumper sticker, or yard sign, and 60 percent or more attend political meetings or campaign rallies, compared to 10 percent and 6 percent of the general public respectively. More than a third of the women's PAC contributors, but just 3 percent of the general public, do other work for candidates or parties, and 62 percent of the women's PAC contributors overall, but only 6 percent of the public, give money to political parties. Six percent of the women's

TABLE 3.1 POLITICAL ACTIVITIES OF WOMEN'S PAC
CONTRIBUTORS AND THE GENERAL PUBLIC (IN PERCENTAGES)

POLITICAL ACTIVITIES	CONTRIBUTORS TO EMILY'S LIST	CONTRIBUTORS TO WISH LIST	CONTRIBUTORS TO S.B. ANTHONY LIST	GENERAL PUBLIC
Talk about campaign	79%	77%	90%	29%
Display campaign button/bumper sticker/sign	53	44	68	10
Attend candidate event	60	74	66	6
Contribute to political party	63	42	66	6
Other party/candidate work	39	44	50	3
Run for political office	6	7	6	—

Sources: Women's PAC Contributor Survey; 1996 American National Election Study.

PAC contributors even run for office themselves. There are some differences in activity level among the three PACs, with The WISH List contributors most likely to attend candidate events and to run for office, and the Anthony List contributors most engaged in all the other activities, but the campaign-related pursuits of all women's PAC donors are uniformly high.

In sum, the major women's PAC contributors are major activists in other ways as well. Scholars and journalists have credited women's PACs, and especially the herculean EMILY's List, with mobilizing a cadre of new donors, women especially, who were previously uninvolved.[14] This may be true of many of the thousands of members who contribute to candidates through the three PACs. But the PACs' $200-plus donors are habitual activists.

Does their commitment grow, the longer they contribute? Studies of other political organizations demonstrate that long-time organization members are less inclined to drop out of the group than are newer members. Most new members know little about a group when they first join, but they gain information quickly once they become involved and learn about the organization from the inside. Some then decide to quit; others like what they learn and stay on. The theory of experiential learning suggests that longer-term members are less likely than new members to learn anything new that would lead them to quit.[15] By extension, it is possible that the commitment of longer-term members may grow as their initial positive impressions are reinforced over time. In the case of PACs, whose primary goal is to raise money for candidates, greater commitment should be most evident in the size of members' contributions.

Many donors to the three women's PACs do give more and participate more as their involvement continues over time. The evidence is mixed, however, and it is strongest in regard to the size of contributions, as expected. Major donors contributed an average of $656 to EMILY's List and $1,473 to The WISH List during the 1995–1996 election cycle; they contributed an average of $853 to the Anthony List during 1998.[16] There is a positive and significant relationship between the number of years that EMILY's List and WISH List donors have contributed and the amount they contributed, but the relationship is neither positive nor significant for the Anthony List donors. The amounts that EMILY's List and WISH List donors report to have given to both the PAC and to its recommended candidates also increase with the number of years of involvement, but again not for the Anthony List donors. Other political activities increase only slightly, if at all, among donors who have contributed to the PACs for a longer time.

In sum, the evidence indicates that getting into the habit of contributing may, over time, lead donors to write larger checks, at least in two out of the three PACs. But for the most part, the primary effect of these women's PACs on their major contributors is neither to mobilize them from passivity nor to motivate increased political activity, but rather to channel financial contributions of actively engaged, affluent donors toward increasing the number of women in elective office who, respectively, are either pro-choice or pro-life.

RECRUITING CONTRIBUTORS THROUGH
SOCIAL NETWORKS AND DIRECT MAIL

EMILY's List began in 1984 as a group of friends and acquaintances, soliciting and bundling candidate contributions; by 1986 it was a formal PAC and it quickly developed a large direct-mail database. The WISH List and the Anthony List began much the same way in the early 1990s. Today, both EMILY's List and the Anthony List rely almost exclusively on direct mail for membership recruitment and retention. The WISH List also uses direct mail, but it relies primarily on events, such as large receptions, breakfasts, and living room gatherings ("like Tupperware parties without the Tupperware") in various states around the country to recruit contributing members.[17] However, a plurality of contributors to the three PACs (44 percent) said they heard about their respective organizations and decided to become involved through friends or acquaintances. Direct mail, at 38 percent, was the second most common way of becoming aware and involved. Only 6 percent said they heard about their organization on the radio or television, and 2 percent by phone. Nine percent heard of the organizations by "other" means; where those others are written in, they refer mostly to other specific people who invited them to join or to attend an event, thus placing them in the friends-and-acquaintances category. All three donor groups also have Web Sites with membership information, and although none of the survey respondents said they learned of the organizations on the World Wide Web, recruitment via the Internet is likely to increase along with rapid growth in Internet usage generally.

There are more direct-mail recruits among EMILY's List and the Anthony List donors than among The WISH List donors, consistent with the organization leaders' perceptions. Overall, EMILY's List contributors (39 percent) and Anthony List contributors (33 percent) were twice as likely as WISH List contributors (19 percent) to learn about the PACs via direct mail. Within each group, more women than men were recruited through personal networks of friends and acquaintances; more men than women were recruited by direct mail (see Table 3.2 on page 40). This is no surprise. All three women's PACs started out as networks of mostly female friends and acquaintances, and most of the personal networking still takes place among women, while mailing lists from a variety of sources include men as well as women.

Organization leaders, especially those of EMILY's List and the Anthony List, say they rely heavily on direct mail to recruit members, yet more donors attribute their involvement to friends and acquaintances than to direct mail. Why the discrepancy? One explanation might be that many survey respondents joined years ago, before direct-mail appeals outpaced friendship networks as methods of organizational outreach. This is a partial explanation at best. EMILY's List contributors who have been involved for ten to fifteen years are indeed twice as likely to have been recruited by friends (72 percent) as are those who have been involved for less time (35 percent). But there

TABLE 3.2   METHODS OF RECRUITMENT AMONG
WOMEN'S PAC CONTRIBUTORS (IN PERCENTAGES)

	CONTRIBUTORS TO EMILY'S LIST		CONTRIBUTORS TO WISH LIST		CONTRIBUTORS TO S.B. ANTHONY LIST	
RECRUITMENT	WOMEN	MEN	WOMEN	MEN	WOMEN	MEN
Direct mail	38%	42%	17%	33%	23%	48%
Friend/acquaintance	44	36	58	56	58	38
Other means	18	22	25	11	19	14
Total	100%	100%	100%	100%	100%	100%

Source: Women's PAC Contributor Survey.

is no relationship between time and recruitment method in the other two groups, nor is there a relationship between time and recruitment method for EMILY's List donors who have been involved fewer than ten years. There is also no clear or significant relationship, within any of the three PACs, between respondents' age and the way they were recruited.

Another explanation for the large number of personal network recruits might be that many members become interested after hearing about the women's PACs through friends and acquaintances, but they do not actually contribute until they receive the direct-mail appeals. In this way, contributors and organization leaders could have different perceptions of how donors de-cide to contribute. Finally, a third possible explanation is that most contribu-tors to the three women's PACs do hear about the organization through direct mail, but the largest contributors—those who give at least $200—are more likely to receive personal solicitations from someone they know. Indeed, pre-vious research has shown that personal solicitation networks tend to collect fewer, but larger, donations, while direct-mail solicitation campaigns attract larger numbers of smaller contributions.[18]

Among the major contributors themselves, interestingly, the contribu-tions of personal network recruits are no larger (and no smaller) than those of direct-mail recruits in any of the three PACs. Nor is there any consistent pat-tern to the political activity levels of personal network recruits versus direct-mail recruits. Previous research on member recruitment in political organizations had found a curvilinear relationship between individuals' ac-tivity level and how they were recruited, with direct-mail recruits tending to be both the least active and the most active. This is because direct mail tends to attract two types of participants: those who are generally uninvolved but who occasionally respond to the simplistic and urgent appeals common in direct-mail solicitations, and those whose opinions are both extreme and aggressive. Personal network recruits, on the other hand, tend to be more moderate both in their attitudes and in their levels of participation.[19] But among the major contributors to the three women's PACs, there is no such discernible relationship, curvilinear or otherwise, between the way contributors were recruited and the number of political activities they undertake. Untapped by the survey, however, is how many times respondents performed each activity. Using such a measure of participation might generate different results, but it would also be of questionable reliability, depending as it would on respondents' memory of every action taken.

Some of the individual activities are related to the method of recruitment in ways that might be expected. Social-network recruits in EMILY's List and The WISH List are more likely than direct-mail recruits to attend candidate events; in EMILY's List they are also more likely to talk to others about the elections and to display a button, bumper sticker, or sign. These are all social activities that might be expected of social-network recruits. Still, there is insufficient evidence that longer periods of association with the PACs or that different methods of recruitment lead to higher levels of political activity. What is clear is that the major contributors to all three women's PACS are far more actively engaged in campaign-related activities than are most citizens.

ORGANIZATIONAL INVOLVEMENTS

In addition to their high degree of electoral activity, contributors belong to a wide variety of political organizations beyond EMILY's List, The WISH List, and the Anthony List. The women's PAC contributor survey asked respondents about membership, as well as dues or contributions and meeting attendance, in fourteen different categories of groups. Only 5 percent of respondents checked none of them. A majority belong to at least four, and the level of organizational involvement is similar for donors across the three PACs. There also are similarities in the types of groups contributors belong to, but there are differences across the three PACs as well (see Table 3.3 on page 42).

More EMILY's List and WISH List contributors belong to business and professional groups than to any other type of group; for Anthony List contributors, the most common type of membership is in church or religious groups. About 60 percent of EMILY's List and WISH List donors belong and contribute to business or professional groups, and close to half of them attend meetings as well, especially those in The WISH List. A substantial minority (40 percent) of the Anthony List donors also belong to business or professional groups. But many more Anthony List donors, over 70 percent, are contributing members of religious groups, compared to about 40 percent of EMILY's List and WISH List donors. Anthony List donors are more than twice as likely as the other two PACs' donors to attend religious group meetings.

TABLE 3.3   SELECTED ORGANIZATIONAL INVOLVEMENT OF WOMEN'S PAC CONTRIBUTORS (IN PERCENTAGES)

TYPE OF ORGANIZATION	MEMBER			GAVE MONEY/ PAID DUES			ATTENDED MEETING/ ACTIVITY		
	EMILY	WISH	ANTHONY	EMILY	WISH	ANTHONY	EMILY	WISH	ANTHONY
Business/professional	61%	59%	40%	59%	58%	38%	40%	47%	34%
Church or religious	39	42	74	42	42	70	29	28	64
Women's rights	53	32	18	62	36	18	17	18	14
Other political issue group	46	28	46	48	32	48	19	23	36
Elderly	18	5	16	21	6	18	4	3	10
Civic or community	48	50	44	50	53	42	33	46	38
Educational or cultural	47	40	42	49	46	44	33	38	28
Service	27	27	44	27	33	44	19	24	30

Source: Women's PAC Contributor Survey.

Anthony List donors also are the most active in service organizations; 44 percent are dues-paying members, compared to 27 percent in the other two women's PACs. But membership in both civic or community groups and in educational or cultural groups is uniformly high; nearly half of the donors to each PAC belong to civic or community groups, and 40 percent or more belong to educational or cultural groups. Conversely, few (under 20 percent) donors to any of the three PACs belong to ethnic, fraternal, children's, or self-help organizations, or to organizations in the "other" category; and almost none of them are labor union members.

Contributors to EMILY's List and to the Anthony List are more likely than those in The WISH List to belong to organizations that focus on other political issues besides abortion; close to half of the first two PACs are involved in other political issue groups, compared to 28 percent in The WISH List. The WISH List contributors are the most politically moderate of the three, with EMILY's List contributors tending toward greater liberalism and Anthony List contributors tending toward greater conservatism. Their relative extremism could provide the impetus for EMILY's List and Anthony List donors to organize around a wider array of political issues. Similarly, EMILY's List and Anthony List donors are more than three times as likely as The WISH List donors to be involved in elderly organizations. Age and retirement status do not fully explain the difference because Anthony List donors are slightly younger and no more likely to be retired than The WISH List donors. At least some of the involvement of EMILY's List and Anthony List donors in elderly groups could be politically motivated, as senior-citizen organizations have become increasingly polarized ideologically in recent decades.[20]

Contributors to the Democratic pro-choice EMILY's List, not surprisingly, are much more involved in women's rights groups than are the other women's PAC contributors. Well over half of the donors to EMILY's List belong or contribute to women's rights organizations, compared to one-third of The WISH List donors and one-sixth of the Anthony List donors. This is consistent, as we will see in subsequent chapters, with the greater propensity of EMILY's List contributors to identify and sympathize with the feminist movement, even though all three PACs share the feminist goal of electing more women to public office.

The organizational connections of political activists carry important implications for a society's political life. Pluralist democratic theory suggests that a polity based on overlapping and competing interest groups encourages moderation and constant negotiation, promoting both flexibility and stability through the participation of diverse interests.[21] Cross-cutting affiliations with diverse social, civic, occupational, and political groups increase people's exposure to a variety of situations and viewpoints, thereby tempering intolerance and extremism. Thus, in a society of individuals with cross-cutting group identifications, majorities are unlikely to run roughshod over minority preferences because individuals will identify with a variety of both majority and minority groups.[22] Conversely, to the extent that the same people join the same narrow range of groups, as a result of like-minded organizations sharing mailing lists for example, prejudices and extreme views will be reinforced rather than tempered.[23] Testing the extent of cross-cutting and overlapping organizational affiliations has been largely anecdotal and speculative due to the lack of data on individuals' multiple memberships.[24] But because the women's PAC contributors are involved in a wide array of organizations, we can at least draw some tentative conclusions about the breadth and extent of overlapping affiliations among these highly committed activists.

The largest differences among the three women's PAC donors lie in their affiliations with political groups and religious groups. Donors to the Susan B. Anthony List are by far the most involved in church or religious groups; donors to EMILY's List are by far the most involved in women's rights groups. This is predictable, given the polarization between the Republican and Democratic parties on abortion and women's rights issues, congruent with the alignments between the Republican party and the religious right on the one hand and with the Democratic party and the feminist movement on the other. In addition, donors to both EMILY's List and the Susan B. Anthony List are much more involved in political issue organizations than are donors to The WISH List. And it is highly unlikely that contributors to the pro-choice Democratic EMILY's List and contributors to the pro-life, mostly Republican Susan B. Anthony List work together often in political issue groups.

Contributors to the three women's PACs do share substantial involvement, however, in business and professional groups, in civic and community groups, in educational and cultural groups, and in service organizations—groups that are generally not overtly political. Not only do they belong and give money to each type of organization; one-third or more attend organization meetings as well. Since the Women's PAC Contributor Survey did not ask about specific organizations, there is no way to know the extent to which contributors belong to the same groups. But such widespread involvement in the same types of groups presents numerous opportunities for common experience and interaction among the contributors to the three women's PACs.

In sum, the patterns of organizational involvement outside of EMILY's List, The WISH List, and the Anthony List represent a mixed bag of potential insulation and interaction among their major contributors. Political alliances may be unlikely among groups with such different partisan loyalties and attitudes toward abortion. But opportunities for interaction nevertheless abound for the major donors with their multiple channels of organization and participation.

CONCLUSION

Major contributors to EMILY's List, The WISH List, and the Anthony List, like major political contributors generally, are well educated, affluent, employed in high-status occupations, highly engaged in electoral politics, and active in a wide variety of organizations. Unlike political contributors generally, however, they are mostly women. Social networks have been important to the growth of all three women's PACs. Although EMILY's List and the Anthony List recruit contributors primarily through direct mail, and The WISH List uses direct mail to supplement its fund-raising events, more contributors to all three PACs say they learned about the groups and decided to become involved through contacts with friends and acquaintances. Although there is little evidence that PAC contributors become more actively engaged in politics through their years of association with the PACs, longer-term members do tend to contribute larger amounts of money. While women's PACs may mobilize new contributors, especially women, to participate in campaign finance, their major contributors—those who give at least $200—are probably politically active to begin with. Thus, the importance of these women's PACs for their major contributors is to channel their efforts in a particular direction: toward electing more women committed to pro-choice or pro-life policies. Contributors recognize this; as one female respondent, active in virtually every aspect of campaigning, states, "[W]ithout EMILY's List educating me [about] the importance of getting women elected to office, I would not be nearly as involved and as large a contributor to Democratic female candidates as I currently am."

Contributors to the three women's PACs share the goal of electing more women, and they may have numerous opportunities to interact through a variety of business and professional, educational and cultural, civic, community, and service groups. But these commonalities will never fully bridge the partisan and ideological divide. The differences and similarities in contributors' partisan loyalties, political attitudes and preferences, and political priorities are explored in the next chapter.

NOTES

1. Calculated by the authors from data available from the Federal Election Commission, as reported by the Center for Responsive Politics on their Web Site, www.opensecrets.org (accessed June 29, 2003).
2. Nonresponses, which are very few on nearly all questions, are coded as missing data in this and subsequent chapters, and thus are not included in the percentages and other statistical calculations.
3. There are, as far as we can tell, no comparable women's PACs that are both pro-life and restricted to candidates of a particular political party.

4. Peter L. Francia, John C. Green, Paul S. Herrnson, Lynda W. Powell, and Clyde Wilcox, *The Financiers of Congressional Elections: Investors, Ideologues, and Intimates* (New York: Columbia University Press, 2004); Benjamin A. Webster, Clyde Wilcox, Paul S. Herrnson, Peter L. Francia, John C. Green, and Lynda W. Powell, "Competing for Cash: The Individual Financiers of Congressional Elections," in *Playing Hardball: Campaigning for the U.S. Congress*, ed. Paul S. Herrnson (Upper Saddle River, NJ: Prentice Hall, 2001); Clifford W. Brown, Jr., Lynda W. Powell, and Clyde Wilcox, *Serious Money: Fundraising and Contributing in Presidential Nomination Campaigns* (New York: Cambridge University Press, 1995).

5. Ibid.

6. U.S. Bureau of Labor Statistics and Bureau of the Census, *CPS Annual Demographic Survey, March Supplement, 1999* (http://ferret.bls.census.gov/macro/031999/hhinc/new01_001.htm).

7. U.S. Bureau of the Census, *Statistical Abstract of the United States: 1999* (http://www.census.gov/prod/99pubs/99statab/sec04.pdf).

8. The figure for the general public is from 1999. U.S. Bureau of the Census, *Statistical Abstract of the United States: 2001* (http://www.census.gov/prod/2001pubs/statab/sec13.pdf).

9. Sidney Verba, Kay Lehman Schlozman, and Henry E. Brady, *Voice and Equality: Civic Voluntarism in American Politics* (Cambridge, MA: Harvard University Press, 1995).

10. Verba, Schlozman, and Brady, *Voice and Equality;* Nancy E. Burns, Kay Lehman Schlozman, and Sidney Verba, *The Private Roots of Public Action: Gender, Equality, and Participation* (Cambridge, MA: Harvard University Press, 2001).

11. This and all other direct quotes attributed to EMILY's List, The WISH List, or Anthony List contributors, unless noted otherwise, come from the final page of the survey on which respondents were invited to write in additional comments.

12. NES data cited in this book are from the following study: Virginia Sapiro, Steven J. Rosenstone, Warren E. Miller, and the National Election Studies, *American National Election Studies, 1948–1997* (CD-ROM), ICPSR ed. (Ann Arbor, MI: Inter-university Consortium for Political and Social Research, producer and distributor, 1998). The collectors, producers, and distributors of the data are not responsible for the analyses and conclusions reported here. It should be noted that 9 percent of the NES respondents are listed as replying "neither" agree nor disagree to the question about people having a say in government, while the survey of women's PAC contributors does not include a "neither," or middle, category.

13. Larry Makinson and the staff of the Center for Responsive Politics, *The Big Picture: The Money behind the 2000 Elections* (Washington, D.C.: The Center for Responsive Politics, 2001), p. 8.

14. Webster, et al., "Competing for Cash," p. 57; Beth Donovan, "Women's Campaigns Fueled Mostly by Women's Checks," *Congressional Quarterly Weekly Report*, 17 October 1992, pp. 3269–3273.

15. Lawrence S. Rothernberg, "Organizational Maintenance and the Retention Decision in Groups," *American Political Science Review* 82 (1988), pp. 1129–1152.

16. The legal limit for individual contributions to PACs is $5,000 per year. The Susan B. Anthony List Candidate Fund, or PAC, was not collecting contributions during 1997. That was the year that the original Anthony List PAC was replaced by a 501(c)(4) educational and political organization; the new affiliated PAC was established the following year, as explained in Chapter 2.

17. Interviews with Ellen R. Malcolm, President, and Sheila O'Connell, Senior Advisor, EMILY's List; Pat Giardina Carpenter, President, The WISH List; and Jennifer Bingham, Executive Director, the Susan B. Anthony List; June 2–10, 2003.

18. Brown, Powell, and Wilcox, *Serious Money*, pp. 140–141.

19. R. Kenneth Godwin, *One Billion Dollars of Influence: The Direct Marketing of Politics* (Chatham, NJ: Chatham House, 1988), pp. 50–66.

20. Christine L. Day, "Old-Age Interest Groups in the 1990s: Coalitions, Competition, and Strategy," in *New Directions in Old Age Policies*, ed. Janie S. Steckenrider and Tonya M. Parrott (Albany, NY: State University of New York Press, 1998).

21. Robert A. Dahl, *A Preface to Democratic Theory* (Chicago: University of Chicago Press, 1956); David B. Truman, *The Governmental Process: Political Interests and Public Opinion* (New York: Knopf, 1951); John S. Sullivan, James Piereson, and George E. Marcus, *Political Tolerance and American Democracy* (Chicago: University of Chicago Press, 1982).

22. Dahl, *A Preface to Democratic Theory*; Robert D. Putnam, "Bowling Alone: America's Declining Social Capital," *Journal of Democracy* 6 (January 1995), pp. 65–78.
23. Godwin, *One Billion Dollars of Influence*; Michael T. Hayes, "Interest Groups: Pluralism or Mass Society?" in *Interest Group Politics*, 1st ed., ed. Allan J. Cigler and Burdett A. Loomis (Washington, D.C.: CQ Press, 1983); Putnam, "Bowling Alone."
24. Frank R. Baumgartner and Jack L. Walker, "Survey Research and Membership in Voluntary Associations," *American Journal of Political Science* 32 (1988), pp. 908–928.

POLITICAL ATTITUDES

CONFLICT AND UNITY AMONG CONTRIBUTORS

EMILY's List, The WISH List, and the Susan B. Anthony List are all in the business of promoting female candidates, but they never promote the same women. EMILY's List and The WISH List support pro-choice female candidates, but candidates of different parties. The WISH List and the Anthony List support Republican female candidates, but candidates with different positions on the abortion issue. And the Anthony List and EMILY's List are the least likely to find common ground. These differences among the three PACs mirror the attitudes of their major contributors, with The WISH List donors generally more moderate on the issues and more ambivalent in their partisanship than the other two donor groups.

EMILY's List and The WISH List both support greater gender equality in politics and abortion rights. But EMILY's List contributors support them mostly from a liberal feminist perspective, a perspective that includes active government promotion of equality and social welfare while opposing governmental intrusion in the realms of religion or individual morality. The WISH List contributors, on the other hand, support gender equality and abortion rights primarily from a laissez-faire conservative perspective, a perspective that also advocates limited government in social welfare and business regulation as well as in morality issues while supporting a strong national defense. Anthony List contributors, finally, support laws prohibiting abortion largely from a socially conservative perspective, a perspective that also promotes governmental intervention in the realms of morality and national defense but not in the areas of social welfare and economic regulation. Thus, The WISH List contributors tend to be closer to those of EMILY's List on social issues such as gender roles, school prayer, gun control, and gay rights, but they are closer to those of the Anthony List on issues related to social welfare, promotion of equality, the role of government, and national defense.

The WISH List contributors also overlap with the other two groups in their political priorities. With EMILY's List donors they share a high degree of concern for improved education and legalized abortion. But they are more similar to those of the Anthony List in their high degree of concern over taxes, public order, and moral decay. In sum, the three donor groups are united by little more than their support for women in government.

POLITICAL PARTIES AND PACS

Relations between PACs and political parties in the United States are complex; sometimes they work in tandem, other times at cross purposes. How do these three women's PACs, each with its relatively narrow focus, interact with the major political parties? EMILY's List and The WISH List are openly partisan while the Anthony List professes bipartisanship while supporting Republicans almost exclusively. Like many political organizations, the three groups perform various functions that political parties perform, not only raising money but also recruiting and training candidates, mobilizing voters, and helping to set the partisan agenda by influencing the party platforms. Thus in many ways such groups help ease the parties' burden while broadening their base of support. At the same time, they can disrupt party unity with unyielding support for certain positions or priorities, as illustrated by the conflict over the abortion issue between supporters of The WISH List and the Anthony List.[1] They also can build interparty coalitions around particular issues, even in the face of increasing partisan polarization, as illustrated by the occasional meetings between leaders of EMILY's List and The WISH List.

Each of the three organizations faces certain political contradictions or criticisms inherent in its partisan and ideological mission. Some detractors charge EMILY's List and The WISH List with having a narrow feminist agenda that shuts out pro-life women and moderate-to-conservative women in general.[2] In the words of one EMILY's List contributor: "I find EMILY's List is too focused—using pro-abortion and being a woman as the criteria for support." And while the Republican WISH List could make a case for itself as the home for more moderate pro-choice women, the group faces its own contradiction: By helping to elect more Republicans, it also helps to expand the power of a party that has officially opposed legal abortion in its presidential platforms for more than twenty years. The Anthony List, finally, encounters the same contradiction faced by other antifeminist and Christian Right groups that are led by female activists: advocating traditional gender roles while at the same time promoting women in nontraditional political leadership roles to make their views more persuasive.[3] Each group in this context must try to maximize its base of support while remaining true to its core principles and retaining the loyalty of its core constituency.

In this chapter we explore the attitudes and priorities of the major contributors to the three women's PACs, highlighting areas of both concurrence and discord. With contributors to The WISH List in between those of the other two groups in most of their issue positions (though not all of them, as we will see), two questions present themselves. First, what are the chances that the two pro-Republican groups, so far apart on the abortion issue, will gradually form a more unified alliance around the conservative issues that they have in common? Second, what are the chances that the two pro-choice groups will gradually form a more unified bipartisan alliance around the issue of abortion and other social or morality issues that they have in common? Or to put it another way, how far apart are The WISH List contributors from EMILY's List contributors on their left and Anthony List contributors on their right in regard to partisan and ideological affinities, issue positions, and political priorities?

With respect to the first question about convergence within the Republican party, previous studies draw different conclusions about the likelihood of greater unity among Republican party activists. One study of donors to Republican party committees and presidential candidates suggests that the long-term prospects are good for full assimilation of the Christian Right, or social conservatives, into the mainstream of the Republican party based on many shared priorities and positions on economic issues.[4] A separate study of conservative female activists, however, draws more skeptical conclusions about a possible close alliance between laissez-faire conservatives, who emphasize free market and property rights, and social conservatives, who emphasize traditional moral values, despite the two groups' common hostility to Big Government and Communism. The individualism and emphasis on self-actualization of the laissez-faire conservatives conflicts with the moral authoritarianism of the social conservatives; this represents a conflict of core values.[5]

We disagree with neither of these conclusions. The conflicts over social issues between the laissez-faire conservatives of The WISH List and the social conservatives of the Anthony List are not likely to dissolve in the face of common goals. Since the Christian Right has become a major constituency of the Republican party, those who are conservative on economic issues but moderate to liberal on social issues, like many of The WISH List contributors, may feel somewhat ambivalent about their partisanship. They have closer potential allies on social issues within the Democratic party and EMILY's List. However, the laissez-faire conservatives of The WISH List and the liberal feminists of EMILY's List are too far apart on issues related to government intervention in social welfare and social equality to become close bipartisan allies. In fact, the days of abortion and gender equality as cross-partisan issues are past, as discussed in Chapter 2; the parties have become increasingly polarized on such issues since the late 1970s. In the following sections we examine in more detail the cleavages among the major contributors to the three women's PACs in their political preferences and priorities.

PARTISANSHIP AND IDEOLOGY AMONG CONTRIBUTORS

In partisanship and in ideology, The WISH List is the group in the middle, but its contributors are closer to those of the Anthony List than to those of EMILY's List: more Republican than Democratic or independent, and more conservative than liberal. Contributors to the Anthony List are overwhelmingly Republican, despite the official bipartisan stance taken by the organization. EMILY's List contributors are the most strongly partisan of the three donor groups.

All of the contributors to EMILY's List are Democrats (except for the 1 percent independents), and 70 percent of them call themselves strong Democrats. All but a handful of contributors to the other two women's PACs are Republicans. Anthony List contributors are the more loyal partisans; 60 percent of them are strong Republicans. Nearly half (47 percent) of The WISH List donors also call themselves strong Republicans. Almost all of the remaining donors to the Anthony List and The WISH List are either weak Republicans or lean Republican; fewer than 6 percent of either group are Democrats, and 7 percent of The WISH List donors (but none in the Anthony List) are independents.

EMILY's List and Anthony List contributors also are more partisan in their donation behavior and in their presidential preferences than are those in The WISH List. Nearly two-thirds of the Anthony List and EMILY's List donors said they contributed money to a political party, compared to just 47 percent of The WISH List donors. Nearly all the contributors to EMILY's List—more than 99 percent—said they supported the Democratic presidential candidate, Bill Clinton, in 1992 and in 1996. At least 85 percent of the Anthony List donors, but only 71 percent of The WISH List donors, supported the Republican presidential candidates in 1992 (George H. W. Bush) and in 1996 (Bob Dole). In sum, while contributors to all three women's PACs are quite strong in their partisanship, those in The WISH List are the most ambivalent of the three— not surprising for the group whose position on the abortion issue deviates from that of the official party platform. Some WISH List donors express that ambivalence in their survey comments about the Republican party, for example: "I like Republicans for all fiscal policies but worry about them as pro-life and too protective about big development." "I am disillusioned with the Republican and Democratic parties as a whole. I look to the individual candidates." "I am a Republican, but that doesn't mean I feel 'warm' toward all Republicans. And, there is a huge difference between 'all Republicans' and 'Republican spokesmen' and 'Republican elected leaders.'"

The WISH List donors are even more moderate in their ideology than in their partisanship. More than half (54 percent) call themselves moderates, while another third are somewhat conservative and 10 percent are somewhat liberal. The other two PACs are ideologically polarized. Nearly half of the Anthony List donors say they are very conservative, and another third say they are somewhat conservative; only 13 percent are moderate and 4 percent are liberal. At the other end of the scale, more than one-third of EMILY's List donors are very liberal and just over half are somewhat liberal; 12 percent are moderate and almost none are conservative.

Once again, some of The WISH List contributors express their preference for moderation and compromise: "To oppose all abortions or to insist on abortions on demand are equally dangerous. . . . To not put the emphasis on prevention distorts the focus. . . . You have the liberals and the conservatives pitted against each other. . . . The true practical working solution is in the middle." "I'd like to see a lot less litmus test issues such as abortion and gay rights, and so on, used in inflammatory ways to polarize the voting public. I'd also like to see much more civility in political debate and more true intellectual content." "Liberals and conservatives ordinarily balance each other. It's the extremists of either group—the lunatic fringe—who cause trouble—violence—sometimes murder—and they are really terrorists. Those who lie and misguide people in the name of religion are the true hypocrites."

Donors to the other two PACs, in contrast, often disparage the other side in their comments, such as the Anthony List donor critical of "the majority [who] are militant feminists, liberal, pro-abortion and believe in tax and spend policies, pro–government regulation, pro–big government," or the EMILY's List donors critical of "the takeover of Congress by Republicans in 1994 [which] was an unmitigated disaster for the country," and "the inroads made by the right wing with their religious social agenda that would rule people according to *their* beliefs."

FEMINIST CONSCIOUSNESS AND SUPPORT FOR WOMEN IN POLITICS

"Feminism," says a slogan of the National Organization for Women, "is the radical notion that women are people." The irony is intentional; who would argue that women are not people? But the concept of feminism means different things to different people; there is no single universally accepted definition or theoretical approach.[6] Feminist consciousness varies from person to person based on their attitudes as well as on their perceptions of what feminism means. Among the contributors to the three women's PACs, feminist consciousness varies in much the same way as partisanship and ideology, with EMILY's List and the Anthony List at the extremes and The WISH List in the middle.

On the surface it may seem that anyone willing to contribute a substantial amount of money to an organization explicitly aimed at increasing women's equality in politics would be a feminist sympathizer. But feminism, as an ideology, goes beyond support for gender equality. Feminism also includes the recognition that the social-political system, not individual women, is to blame for women's disadvantaged status; and it includes a belief in the need for collective action to bring about social change favoring women's rights.[7] Our measure of feminist consciousness incorporates these beliefs by combining two elements: (1) feminist self-identification; and (2) the relative feeling thermometer score for the women's movement, an indicator of support for collective action in favor of women's rights. The possible scores on the feminist consciousness scale range from –2 to 4.33.[8]

EMILY's List contributors are extremely high on the feminist consciousness scale, averaging 4.17, which is just short of the highest possible score and significantly higher than contributors to the other two women's PACs (see Table 4.1). The WISH List contributors average almost an entire point lower on the feminism scale; Anthony List contributors are much lower still, averaging more than two full points lower than those in The WISH List. Feminist consciousness, not surprisingly, is highest in the Democratic pro-choice group; it is by far the lowest in the pro-life group. Feminist self-identification follows the same pattern: When respondents are asked whether they think of themselves as feminists, most EMILY's List donors reply "most of the time" or "some of the time"; most Anthony List donors reply "occasionally" or "never"; and WISH List donors are in the middle. At the same time, there is almost no difference among the three groups of contributors in their self-identification as homemakers, or as working women or working men (see Table 4.1). Those who think of themselves as working women or men most of the time comprise about 60 percent of each group; most-of-the-time homemakers account for around 18 percent of each group.

How do contributors to the two pro-Republican PACs reconcile their antifeminist attitudes, particularly strong among the Anthony List, with their

TABLE 4.1   SELF-IDENTIFICATION AND FEMINIST
CONSCIOUSNESS AMONG WOMEN'S PAC CONTRIBUTORS

	EMILY's List Mean Scores	WISH List Mean Scores	F-EMILY's vs. WISH List	Anthony List Mean Scores	F-Anthony vs. WISH List
Feminist consciousness	4.17	3.25	88.92[*]	1.05	59.84[*]
Feminist self-identification	3.67	2.98	88.69[*]	1.73	40.22[*]
Homemaker self-identification	2.39	2.25	1.33	2.45	.84
Worker self-identification	3.38	3.48	1.04	3.43	.09

The F value in this and subsequent tables is a test of significant difference between group means.
[*]p < .001.
Source: Women's PAC Contributor Survey.

support for greater women's equality in politics? Anthony List donors explain: "Women are the backbone of the conservative and pro-life movements." "Women should be involved in all endeavors they are qualified to do. We should remember that the most notable occupation is that of mother and household executive." "Women have a great opportunity to add to politics in this century. They can add a different viewpoint to the discussion and can bring politics back to a more respectable profession with better collegiality. However, to date many of the women in politics are not truly feminine but rather hard-nosed, hard-line feminists. I think this lowers the quality of the caliber of politicians. . . . Women should be women, not men." "The perceived, and often actual, denigration by feminists of the roles of wife and mother, the insistence that women are victimized by 'male chauvinists,' 'suits,' and Catholic and other anti-abortion clergy, and the high rate of homosexuality and bisexuality among feminist leaders, have created a new genre of young American women whose mantra is: 'I am not a feminist.'" Yet another Anthony List contributor identifies herself as a feminist while at the same time critiquing the mainstream feminist movement: "I was a pioneer thirty-two years ago in building a business while raising children and maintaining a home and marriage. It is not popular to speak of or fight for the core values which I hold dear. I respect deeply women who are political pioneers, speaking out for traditional values which elevate and benefit women. That is why I support pro-life feminism." These comments help explain the Anthony List paradox of working to elect more women to offices long dominated by men, while at the same time promoting traditional notions of gender roles and gender behavior.

The WISH List contributors' beliefs about the need to elect more women are congruent with their laissez-faire attitudes emphasizing personal responsibility and nondiscrimination over group-based collective action: "I'm a strong believer in the desirability of the best individual to do the job—gender, race, and so on, are immaterial; capability and conformity to my beliefs are the criteria by which I judge and contribute time, dollars, and endorsements." "As for women in politics, they are doing fine and should have been there long ago. But the issues of who needs extra governmental services should be those with the *need*, not those of a race, a gender, a sex orientation and certainly not the bureaucrats, teachers, and so on, running the programs that fail to help those with the needs."

These comments contrast with the views of contributors to EMILY's List. Their comments evoke two major themes about electing women: (1) that women are not properly represented in a male-dominated government, and (2) that female officials have something special to offer in politics both substantively and stylistically. Illustrative of the first theme are the following: "I think we have a lot of power and I hope more women realize this and become politically active. We can make a difference and if more women run for public office we can replace the male lawyers who don't think like the rest of the nation—they are out of touch!" "Women are no better than men but we have a different biological and cultural experience in society and thus need our voices represented by women in political and other roles. I need to see my faces in Congress! That's what moved me to join EMILY's List—seeing all those white men in blue suits and red ties coming out of the Congress building one day. They don't represent me." Illustrative of the second theme are these: "Women are a good influence in politics. They are more interested in children, health, and education. Their leadership style is more consensus building." "We need more women in politics. They are more sensitive to the issues." "I appreciate the compassionate leaning of most women in politics." "I think that most women have a more rational, sensitive approach to social issues than do many men." "I truly believe that women make the difference. They run for a chance to get the job done rather than stroke an ego. For the most part in legislatures and executive office they are more progressive than men and want to solve conflict rather than promote it. These women overall also have much higher ethical standards." "We will have a more just and egalitarian society when women and other minorities are involved in politics." "As the father of two young women, I believe in gender politics; as an ex-lawyer, I believe in making sure we do not have a conservative judiciary and as a humanist I think white males are out of control!!!" Finally, one woman who contributes to EMILY's List sums up her feelings: "Of course I am a feminist. I think, therefore I am a feminist."

CONTRIBUTORS' POLICY PRIORITIES AND PREFERENCES

Beyond the goal of electing more women to political office, the political priorities and preferences of contributors to the three women's PACs diverge, reflecting their partisan and ideological affinities. EMILY's List and Anthony List donors hold the most disparate and polarized attitudes, with The WISH List donors expressing more moderate views and sharing some of the other two groups' major priorities.

The attitudes of the typical EMILY's List contributor represent liberal feminism: concern for social and economic equality and for reducing poverty, and support for collective action and governmental effort in addressing the needs of the disadvantaged.[9] Both laissez-faire conservatives and social conservatives oppose much of the liberal feminist vision, but on such different grounds that conflicts also arise between these two conservative groups. Social conservatism—represented in this study by Anthony List contributors—is rooted in religious belief, and it is most concerned with preserving the traditional family, upholding traditional moral values, and addressing such social issues as abortion, homosexuality, changing gender roles, and school prayer. Feminism is opposed outright as a force of moral decay and intrusive government, and as a threat to the family unit and therefore to society as a whole. Laissez-faire conservatism—represented in this study by WISH List contributors—is rooted in classical liberalism, and it is most concerned with protecting individual freedom and the free enterprise system, as well as maintaining a strong national defense and the U.S. role as world leader. Laissez-faire conservatives generally support the feminist goal of gender equality in the name of equal individual opportunity, but they oppose government intervention to regulate business or promote equality.[10]

POLITICAL PRIORITIES

Contributors' responses to the question, "What do you think is the most important problem facing this country?" illustrate the polarization between EMILY's List and the Anthony List, and the ways in which The WISH List overlaps with each of the other two. Education is the major concern for the largest number of contributors to EMILY's List (18 percent) and The WISH List (19 percent). Beyond the education issue, however, the two groups diverge in their priorities. Economic inequality, health care, overpopulation, and environmental problems round out the top issues that EMILY's List donors consider to be most important (see Table 4.2). Two of the next three biggest concerns for WISH List donors, on the other hand, match two of the top three issues for Anthony List donors: crime/violence/public order, and moral or religious decay. The latter, however, is overwhelmingly the top priority for Anthony List contributors; 48 percent of them cite moral or religious decay as the nation's most important problem, compared to close to 6 percent of The WISH List contributors. Furthermore, about another 6 percent of The WISH List contributors feel that the most important problem is too much religious intrusion into government and politics—something that presumably does not bother the religious conservatives of the Anthony List. Abortion is second on the list of most important problems (12 percent), after moral decay, for Anthony List donors.

When respondents are asked to rank various issues as to their importance in influencing their vote, the abortion issue ranks among the highest for contributors to all three women's PACs. But for the two pro-Republican donor groups, tax reduction is the other high-priority issue. For EMILY's List donors, the other high-priority issues besides abortion are related to social welfare, equality, women's rights, and the environment, all of which rate very low for contributors to The WISH List and the Susan B. Anthony List. The WISH List donors rate the conservative-agenda issues of taxes, defense, and trade significantly higher than do EMILY's List donors; they rate the liberal-agenda issues of gender, AIDS, and the environment significantly higher than do Anthony List donors. Table 4.3 on page 58 displays the mean importance of each issue (based on a five-point scale) for contributors to each of the three women's PACs.

Despite the centrality of the abortion issue for all three PACs in deciding which candidates to support, none of the contributors to either of the

TABLE 4.2   MOST IMPORTANT PROBLEM FACING THIS COUNTRY (IN PERCENTAGES)

EMILY'S LIST RESPONDENTS		THE WISH LIST RESPONDENTS		ANTHONY LIST RESPONDENTS	
Education	17.5%	Education	19.3%	Moral/religious decay	48.0%
Economic inequality	14.2	Crime/violence/public order	6.8	Abortion	12.0
Health/medical care	6.6	Moral/religious decay	5.7	Crime/violence/public order	8.0
Overpopulation	4.2	Religion too political/School prayer	5.7	Youth/family problems	4.0
Environment/ecology	4.1	Health/medical care	4.5	Education	4.0
Crime/violence/public order	3.8	Taxes	4.5	All others	10.0
Public apathy	3.4	Government too powerful	4.5	No answer	14.0
All others	31.2	Public apathy	3.4		
No answer	15.0	All others	34.2		
		No answer	11.4		

Note: Problems receiving at least 3 percent (3%) of the mentions are listed in the table.
Source: Women's PAC Contributor Survey.

TABLE 4.3   IMPORTANCE OF ISSUE TO VOTE (MEAN SCORES)

Policy Area	EMILY's List	WISH List	F-EMILY's vs. WISH List	Anthony List	F-Anthony vs. WISH List
Tax policy	2.78	1.64	89.16**	1.80	.81
Gender issues	1.70	2.52	48.67**	3.63	17.45**
Health care	1.62	2.49	79.91**	2.63	.41
National defense	2.88	2.21	36.92**	2.02	.87
Affirmative action	2.19	2.89	41.67**	2.95	.06
Environmental policy	1.80	2.62	64.82**	3.05	3.29
Abortion	1.28	1.73	29.14**	1.22	8.37*
Gay rights	2.01	3.13	97.17**	2.71	2.32
Jobs	2.14	2.65	20.79**	3.10	3.03
Race issues	1.96	3.06	96.40**	3.13	.08
AIDS policy	2.54	3.59	76.61**	4.10	4.76
Trade policy	2.69	2.30	9.11*	2.63	2.05

Note: Responses range from 1 = most important to 5 = least important.
*p < .01   **p < .001
Source: Women's PAC Contributor Survey.

pro-choice PACs cite abortion policy as the nation's most important problem, in contrast to 12 percent of the Anthony List respondents. The centrality of fighting abortion dominates many of the voluntary comments offered by Anthony List contributors, while EMILY's List and WISH List donors mention the abortion issue less often in their comments—and then, in somewhat ambivalent terms or in the broader context of individual rights. Observe, for example, these comments from EMILY's List donors—"Abortion is neither the only nor the most important item on the agenda; consider pay equity, equal opportunity for sports . . . separation of church and state;" "No one is *for* abortion! I am against abortion, however I feel only a female has the right to choose"—and from a WISH List donor—"Abortions are a violent procedure; multiples can inflict permanent damage. I would love to see the 'anti's' recommend contraception; that's why I have such a low opinion of the Catholic Church." The Anthony List donors' comments about the abortion issue display a higher degree of moral certainty and single-issue focus, for example: "Abortion has set women and social problems back." "[The abortion] issue almost in and of itself created the antifeminism of today and led to the growth of the pro-life women's political movement." "I love the liberal stance on the environment, health care, protecting labor jobs, and so on, but I hate abortion. . . . I think abortion is an abomination for which we make the God of the Universe cry."

POLICY PREFERENCES

The broad ideological differences among the three groups of contributors translate into differences of opinion on a wide range of policies, revealing once again the relative moderation of The WISH List donors compared to the other two groups. On fifteen out of seventeen issues presented in the survey, the mean responses of WISH List contributors lie between the means for the more liberal EMILY's List and the more conservative Anthony List. The two exceptions are the death penalty and the military force issues; on these two issues, WISH List contributors are the most conservative of the three groups, most likely to favor both the use of the death penalty and the use of military force abroad (see Table 4.4 on page 60).

While The WISH List donors tend to be less extreme in their policy preferences than donors to the other two PACs, they tend to be closer to EMILY's List donors on the social or morality issues and closer to Anthony List donors on social welfare and equality issues, as would be expected of laissez-faire conservatives. With their emphasis on individual liberty and an unfettered free market, the laissez-faire conservatives of The WISH List are closer to the Anthony List donors in their attitudes toward equality, social welfare, and the environment; both groups strongly oppose the government efforts supported by EMILY's List donors. Statistically, WISH List and Anthony List donors are identical in their opposition to affirmative action, government provision of jobs or health care, and big government in general; they also are equally supportive of higher defense spending. At the same time, the penchant of WISH List donors for individual liberty places them closer to EMILY's List donors on the social issues of abortion, women's equality, gay rights, school prayer, and handgun control, as both groups strongly oppose the governmental imposition of moral authority supported by Anthony List donors, and they support the regulation of gun ownership opposed by Anthony List donors. The WISH List and EMILY's List donors are virtually identical in their support for legalized abortion, their belief that mothers of young children need not stay at home rather than take a job, and their relatively high opposition to the use of military force abroad (see Table 4.4 on page 60).

In multivariate analyses exploring the sources of policy disagreements, ideological and partisan differences emerge as the dominant factors explaining issue differences between The WISH List and EMILY's List donors, and between The WISH List and the Anthony List donors. Social status variables including religion, occupation, gender, age, and marital status add nothing to the explanation of policy differences between contributors to the two prochoice donor groups. But religious variables do help to explain policy attitude differences between The WISH List and the Anthony List donors on many of the social issues—the types of issues on which Anthony List donors are significantly to the right of WISH List donors. Respondents who agree with the statement, "the Bible is God's word and all it says is true"—65 percent of Anthony List donors but only 10 percent of WISH List donors—tend

TABLE 4.4 POLICY PREFERENCES (MEAN SCORES)

POLICY STATEMENT	EMILY's LIST	WISH LIST	F-EMILY's vs. WISH LIST	ANTHONY LIST	F-ANTHONY vs. WISH LIST
Government improve women's situation	1.34	1.93	82.57**	2.64	18.65**
Make abortion legal	1.09	1.14	2.61	3.94	2151.78**
No increase in defense spending	1.71	2.72	184.82**	2.96	2.53
Don't reduce domestic spending in order to cut taxes	1.24	2.32	319.19**	2.87	11.45*
No prayer in public schools	1.45	2.28	103.19**	3.22	34.30**
Government improve blacks' social/economic position	1.47	2.29	154.29**	2.65	5.89
Ban the sale of handguns	1.50	2.06	36.12**	3.38	63.29**
Increase spending on environmental protection	1.50	2.31	147.81**	2.93	17.57**
Government guarantee job/good standard of living	2.39	3.29	114.01**	3.50	3.33
Women equal role in business, industry, government	1.25	1.48	20.95**	2.09	21.28**
Government provide low cost doctors, health care	1.63	2.65	216.81**	2.94	3.13
Preference in hiring and promotion for blacks	2.36	3.28	124.07**	3.46	1.70
United States should not be willing to use military force	2.59	2.79	6.52	2.19	15.90**
Government protect homosexuals from discrimination	1.50	2.19	82.00**	3.36	55.47**
No death penalty for murderers	2.08	3.33	155.72**	2.57	22.15**
Mothers with small children need not remain at home	1.67	1.83	4.76	3.00	64.31**
Government not involved in things people should do themselves	1.87	3.33	382.21**	3.43	.53

Note: Responses coded as follows: 1 = Strongly Agree, 2 = Agree, 3 = Disagree, 4 = Strongly Disagree; some recoded appropriately so that low scores represent the liberal responses.

*p < .01 **p < .001

Source: Women's PAC Contributor Survey.

to be more strongly opposed to abortion, more favorable toward school prayer and defense spending, and more likely to believe that mothers with small children should not work outside the home. Roman Catholics—56 percent of Anthony List donors but only 5 percent of WISH List donors—tend to be more strongly opposed to both legalized abortion and the death penalty.[11]

There are two issues on which The WISH List donors are at one extreme rather than in between the other two groups. They are most likely to favor the use of the death penalty, which EMILY's List donors are most likely to oppose. The WISH List donors also are the most favorable toward the use of military force abroad, while Anthony List donors are the most isolationist in the use of military force. Although the Anthony List contributors are consistently the most conservative on all other issues, their relatively moderate position on the death penalty likely reflects the religious views held by many Anthony List donors on the meaning and sanctity of life. Roman Catholicism is the only significant variable in a multivariate analysis of WISH List and Anthony List donor attitudes toward the death penalty,[12] perhaps a reflection of U.S. Catholic clergy's routine condemnation of capital punishment.[13]

The Anthony List contributors' strong opposition to the use of military force abroad, even as they support increased defense spending more than the other two groups, may reflect the foreign-policy views of the Christian Right: generally isolationist, but at the same time supportive of a strong defense against any potential foreign intervention.[14] But unlike virtually all of the other issues, attitudes toward the use of force are not significantly related to ideological or partisan self-identification among any of the three contributor groups. This absence of any clear link between ideology and support for military intervention must be viewed in the context of foreign and military policy at the time of the contributor survey—post-Cold War and pre-September 11, 2001—when the most publicized U.S. military action abroad occurred in the Balkans, most notably Kosovo. Attitudes toward the use of military force were in flux, generally less partisan and more complex than they were before the fall of the Soviet Union and after the 2001 terrorist attacks on New York City and Washington, D.C.

CONCLUSION

Support for women in politics stretches across ideological and partisan lines; many antifeminists now embrace the once-radical feminist notion that politics is not just a man's world. Political organizations that support female candidates also extend across ideological and partisan lines, as illustrated by the liberal feminist attitudes of EMILY's List contributors, the laissez-faire conservative attitudes of WISH List contributors, and the socially conservative attitudes of Susan B. Anthony List contributors.

The WISH List was founded with the help and cooperation of EMILY's List leaders sharing the goal of electing more pro-choice women. They both repudiate the social conservative vision of a society steeped in traditional values and subject to moral authority. But their major contributors are unlikely to form a close political alliance across political party lines; they are too antagonistic in their attitudes toward collective action and governmental responsibility for promoting equality, civil rights, and social welfare.

At the same time, a close alliance among major contributors to the two pro-Republican PACs is also unlikely. While major contributors to the pro-choice WISH List and the pro-life Anthony List are united in their opposition to the liberal feminist vision of EMILY's List donors, they remain divided over political priorities and over the role of government in imposing certain religious moral values. Furthermore, laissez-faire, pro-business fiscal conservatives, represented by The WISH List, form the backbone of the Republican party traditionally. But contributors to the Anthony List, associated with the socially conservative wing of the party, generally exhibit greater party loyalty in terms of partisan identification, financial support, and presidential choice.

As for potential relations between EMILY's List and the Anthony List, opposition to the death penalty could unite some social conservatives of the Republican party with liberal feminists of the Democratic party. But one issue, even one as currently salient as capital punishment, is a highly improbable basis for a broad alliance.

EMILY's List, The WISH List, and the Susan B. Anthony List are united in their mission to get more women elected to public office. Contributors to The WISH List, the more moderate of the three groups, share some political attitudes and priorities with EMILY's List contributors on their left, and they share other attitudes and priorities with the Anthony List contributors on their right. But overall, the bases for cooperation among major contributors to any two of the three women's PACs are slim, while the divisions among them are largely unsurmountable and fundamentally ideological.

NOTES

1. Paul S. Herrnson, *Congressional Elections: Campaigning at Home and in Washington*, 4th ed. (Washington, D.C.: CQ Press, 2004), Chapters 4 and 5; Mark J. Rozell, "Helping Women Run and Win: Feminist Groups, Candidate Recruitment and Training," *Women and Politics* 21 (2000), pp. 101–116; Mark J. Rozell and Clyde Wilcox, *Interest Groups in American Campaigns* (Washington, D.C.: CQ Press, 1999).
2. Eliza Newlin Carney, "Weighing In," *National Journal*, 13 June 1992, pp. 1399–1403; Eliza Newlin Carney, "A New Breed of 'Feminist,'" *National Journal*, 26 March 1994, pp. 728–729.
3. Sara Diamond, *Not By Politics Alone: The Enduring Influence of the Christian Right* (New York: The Guilford Press, 1998), p. 127.
4. John C. Green and James C. Guth, "The Christian Right in the Republican Party: The Case of Pat Robertson's Supporters," *Journal of Politics* 50 (1988), pp. 150–165.
5. Rebecca Klatch, *Women of the New Right* (Philadelphia, PA: Temple University Press, 1987).
6. For an excellent introduction to the various theoretical approaches to feminism, see Rosemary Putnam Tong, *Feminist Thought: A More Comprehensive Introduction*, 2nd ed. (Boulder, CO:

Westview, 1998); Valerie Bryson, *Feminist Debates: Issues of Theory and Political Practice* (New York: New York University Press, 1999); Carolyn Allen and Judith A. Howard, eds., *Provoking Feminisms* (Chicago: University of Chicago Press, 2000).

7. Claire Knoche Fulenwider, *Feminism in American Politics: A Study of Ideological Influence* (New York: Praeger, 1980); Ethel Klein, *Gender Politics: From Consciousness to Mass Politics* (Cambridge, MA: Harvard University Press, 1984); Virginia Sapiro, *The Political Integration of Women: Role, Socialization, and Politics* (Urbana, IL: University of Illinois Press, 1983).

8. The feminist consciousness scale is an additive one combining the relative feeling thermometer score, ranging from –1 to 2.33, and the four-point feminist self-identification score, recoded to range from –1 (never think of self as feminist) to 2 (think of self as feminist most of the time). The relative feeling thermometer score is calculated by subtracting the respondent's mean feeling thermometer score for several groups from the women's movement feeling thermometer score, then dividing it by the mean score for the several groups (score – mean/mean). This corrects for response bias that could contaminate a measure based solely on the women's movement feeling thermometer score. In our own calculation, the respondents' mean feeling thermometer scores are based on feelings toward conservatives, liberals, environmentalists, abortion opponents, abortion supporters, labor unions, the Catholic Church, big business, people on welfare, older people, Christian fundamentalists, blacks, whites, the military, lesbians/gays, Democrats, and Republicans, in addition to the women's movement. See Appendix B, 3h, for the feeling thermometer question wording. See Elizabeth Adell Cook, "Measuring Feminist Consciousness," *Women and Politics* 9 (1989), pp. 71–88 on the relative feeling thermometer and other issues regarding the measurement of feminism. See also Pamela Johnston Conover, "Feminists and the Gender Gap," *Journal of Politics* 50 (1988), pp. 985–1010 on the measurement of feminist consciousness.

9. Fulenwider, *Feminism in American Politics*; Klein, *Gender Politics*.

10. Klatch, *Women of the New Right*.

11. For more on the analysis of attitudinal differences between contributors to EMILY's List and The WISH List, see Christine L. Day and Charles D. Hadley, "Feminist Diversity: The Policy Preferences of Women's PAC Contributors," *Political Research Quarterly* 54 (2001), pp. 673–686. For more on the analysis of attitudinal differences between contributors to the Anthony List and The WISH List, see Charles D. Hadley and Christine L. Day, "Electing Women to National Public Office: Partisanship and Ideology in Women's PACs," presented at the annual meeting of the American Political Science Association, August 30–September 2, 2001, San Francisco, CA. Both studies employ ordinary least squares regression analysis to estimate the independent effects of various partisan, ideological, and social factors on policy attitudes.

12. Hadley and Day, "Electing Women to National Public Office."

13. Joe Soss, Laura Langbein, and Alan R. Metelko, "Why Do White Americans Support the Death Penalty?" *Journal of Politics* 65 (2003), pp. 397–421.

14. Green and Guth, "The Christian Right in the Republican Party."

FEMALE AND MALE CONTRIBUTORS

A GENDER GAP?

Women are the minority in most studies of political contributors, about 40 percent of political contributors generally, and 25 percent of those who give $200 or more in a single election cycle.[1] Men, in contrast, are a small minority in this study of women's PAC contributors. Men comprise just 6 percent of EMILY's List respondents, 10 percent of The WISH List respondents, and 46 percent of Anthony List respondents. Who are these men who contribute substantial amounts of money to help women win elections? Are they as strongly feminist in orientation as their female counterparts—or perhaps even more so, given the absence of group or self-interest in supporting candidates of the opposite sex? Do the women and men in this female-dominated population of contributors demonstrate the same attitudinal gender gaps found in previous studies of political activists? In this chapter we take a closer look at the men, and the similarities and differences between the women and the men who contribute to EMILY's List and to the Anthony List, in order to answer these questions.

The number of male respondents in EMILY's List and in the Anthony List is sufficiently large to enable comparisons across gender lines within each group. Anthony List donors are nearly evenly divided by gender, yielding a sufficient number of both women and men for analysis. EMILY's List donors are overwhelmingly women, but the male oversample, obtained by surveying all of the men who contributed to EMILY's List, also yields a sufficient number of men as well as women for analysis. There are so few men among The WISH List donors that it is impossible to study them or to compare them systematically with the women.

Gender differences are minimal within each PAC, compared to the wide gulf that separates EMILY's List and Anthony List contributors. But a few significant gender differences do emerge that are consistent with previous findings in the gender gap literature. First, within each PAC, women are somewhat more liberal; men are somewhat more conservative. That is, among the major contributors to EMILY's List, the women are slightly more liberal and slightly more Democratic than are the men; among the major contributors to the Anthony List, the men are slightly more conservative and slightly more Republican than are the women. Second, within each PAC, the men tend to be more conservative than the women on use of force issues such as gun control and national defense. Third, the women of EMILY's List are generally more supportive of feminist principles than are the men of EMILY's List, although there is no such gender gap in attitudes toward feminism among Anthony List contributors. We conclude that male contributors to EMILY's List are less driven by feminist consciousness than women to contribute; instead, they are motivated by a more general commitment to egalitarianism. Both the male and female contributors to the Anthony List, on the other hand, are similarly motivated by social conservatism.

GENDER AND ATTITUDES AMONG POLITICAL ACTIVISTS

Women tend to take a more liberal stance than men on a wide variety of issues from social welfare and national defense to environmental regulation and gun control, according to several studies of the general public.[2] Similar gender differences have been found in the attitudes and political priorities of government officials and party activists.[3] However, findings about gender differences among political elites and activists have varied somewhat across populations and across time.

Prior to the 1980s there was almost no gender gap in political attitudes among party elites and elected officials.[4] By the late 1980s, however, female politicians and activists were quite consistently more liberal than their male counterparts in several policy areas ranging from social welfare and government regulation to defense, crime and punishment, and women's rights. Often the gender gap among elites is wider than that among the general public, especially on women's equality and reproductive issues.[5] Female elites increasingly distinguished themselves from their male peers as their numbers grew to a critical mass, at which point they could form effective women's caucuses and develop a sense of solidarity around women's rights and women's priorities.[6] Yet this trend toward solidarity and distinctiveness among female political elites has been tempered, even more recently, as women are recruited from a broader base. Legislative women's caucuses, for example, have a harder time reaching consensus when the women in them range from liberal Democrats to conservative Republicans, profeminist to antifeminist, pro-choice to antichoice.[7]

Although female activists and politicians are somewhat more likely to be drawn from the Democratic party than from the Republican party, their relative liberalism compared to male elites is not fully explained by their partisanship. Female elites tend to be more liberal than their male counterparts on many issues within each political party.[8] Another study of political contributors found Democratic women to be more liberal than Democratic men in their policy preferences, and Republican women to be more conservative than Republican men. However, once religious variables were controlled for, Republican women also were more liberal than the men in their party.[9]

Explaining the gender gap in political attitudes and behavior poses a complex puzzle that researchers are still piecing together. One set of explanations centers around inherent gender differences in psychology and morality, stemming from gender-role socialization and perhaps even biology. Because of the way women and men are socialized, women are more likely than men to have hands-on caregiving experience within the family, and those who work outside the home are also more likely than men to work in caregiving occupations such as nursing, child care, elder care, or social work. Women's approach to conflict or problem-solving tends to be context-sensitive, nurturing, and cooperative, while men's approach is more geared toward justice, impersonal rules, and abstract rights.[10] Gender differences in life experiences both inside and outside the home may contribute to women's relatively stronger support for government efforts in social welfare, promotion of equality, environmental protection, and consumer safety. Even more pervasive over time and after controlling for other factors is women's greater opposition to the use of force, both domestically and internationally. Women are more likely, for example, to support gun control and to oppose capital punishment, higher defense spending and military intervention abroad.[11]

Women's relatively lower socioeconomic status and their higher poverty rate also may contribute to their more liberal views. Socioeconomic variables, however, have generally had little or no explanatory effect on gender differences in attitudes, especially among political activists, who tend to be relatively well educated and comfortable financially.[12] Variation in socioeconomic status is especially low among respondents to the women's PAC contributor survey; more than 80 percent have annual incomes over $80,000, nearly all have college degrees, and most have postgraduate degrees.

Feminist consciousness also may help to explain gender gaps in political attitudes. Women who are feminists have been found to differ significantly from men on a wide range of political values and domestic and foreign-policy issues, where no difference was found between nonfeminist women and men. This suggests that a woman's perspective is more likely to emerge among women who experience a sense of feminist identity and consciousness.[13] In addition, the feminist movement has helped increase women's economic and psychological autonomy with respect to men, encouraging a more independent and differentiated political perspective as well.[14] Political activists expressing feminist views and values do indeed tend to hold more liberal and egalitarian views, but this is true of the men as well as the women.[15]

In short, each of the explanations for the gender gap in political attitudes and behavior is a partial explanation at best. The findings in the following sections show that the differences between the PACs are much greater than the differences between the women and men within each PAC. But the gender gaps that do emerge are in the expected direction, with female contributors to each PAC somewhat more liberal, more averse to force and violence, and among EMILY's List contributors, more feminist, than their male counterparts.

IDEOLOGY AND PARTISANSHIP

Major contributors to EMILY's List are nearly all Democrats and self-described liberals; major contributors to the Anthony List are nearly all Republicans and self-described conservatives. This is true of both the women and the men who contribute to each PAC, with little variation by sex in either group. But, consonant with previous studies of political activists and elites, the women in EMILY's List are slightly more liberal and strongly Democratic than the men; and the women in the Anthony List are slightly less conservative and less strongly Republican than the men.

Nearly the same percentage of EMILY's List women (70 percent) and EMILY's List men (68 percent) call themselves strong Democrats. But 7 percent of the men, compared to only 1 percent of the women, consider themselves independents; the rest are either weak Democrats or are independents leaning Democratic. Similarly, EMILY's List women are a few percentage points more likely than the men to call themselves very liberal (36 to 35 percent) or somewhat liberal (52 to 49 percent), while the men are a bit more likely than the women to be either moderate or even conservative (17 to 13 percent).

Gender differences in partisanship and ideology are slightly larger in the Anthony List than in EMILY's List. In fact, there is a difference of almost 20 percentage points in strong partisans; 71 percent of the men in the Anthony List say they are strong Republicans, compared to just 52 percent of the women. Ideologically, Anthony List women are somewhat more likely than the men to be very conservative (52 to 48 percent), but they also are more likely than the men to say they are moderates (16 to 5 percent), while twice as many men as women say they are somewhat conservative (48 to 24 percent). In addition, two of the Anthony List women (8 percent)—but none of the men—say they are both liberal and strongly Democratic even though they believe abortion should not be legal. The relative moderation of Anthony List women compared to the men exists even without controlling for the women's higher degree of religiosity.

Overall, while the gender differences are small, the women in each PAC are slightly more liberal, or less conservative, and more Democratic, or less Republican, than the men. These differences manifest themselves more clearly in responses to some of the questions about specific issues and priorities. Table 5.1 on page 68 displays the mean policy preferences for female and male contributors to both EMILY's List and the Anthony List, and it shows which issues produce a significant gender gap within each PAC.

TABLE 5.1 WOMEN'S AND MEN'S POLICY PREFERENCES AMONG CONTRIBUTORS TO EMILY'S LIST AND SUSAN B. ANTHONY LIST

POLICY STATEMENT	EMILY'S LIST			SUSAN B. ANTHONY LIST		
	WOMEN'S MEAN	MEN'S MEAN	F	WOMEN'S MEAN	MEN'S MEAN	F
Feminism/Women's Rights						
Feminism scale	4.20	3.55	85.58***	1.27	.80	1.66
Women equal role in business, industry, government	1.25	1.38	13.62***	1.96	2.26	1.17
Government improve women's situation	1.34	1.40	1.31	2.54	2.79	.65
Abortion	1.09	1.11	.69	4.00	3.86	2.24
Mothers with small children work outside home	1.67	1.73	1.35	3.10	2.84	1.18
Equality						
Cut spending to cut taxes	1.23	1.36	9.43**	2.79	3.05	.79
Government improve blacks' social/economic position	1.47	1.45	.34	2.63	2.75	.22
Government guarantee job/standard of living	2.39	2.31	1.44	3.46	3.57	.36
Government provide low-cost doctors, health care	1.64	1.56	2.25	2.83	3.09	.90
Preference in hiring and promotion for blacks	2.37	2.28	1.69	3.57	3.36	.95
Government protect homosexuals from discrimination	1.50	1.52	.06	3.32	3.43	.18
Government involved in things people should do themselves	1.88	1.73	5.88*	3.32	3.57	1.29
Militarism/Use of Force						
United States use military force	2.57	2.77	10.40**	2.04	2.38	1.54
Death penalty for murder	2.07	2.21	3.30	2.36	2.86	2.37
Defense spending	1.71	1.78	1.46	2.92	3.05	.27
Handgun ban	1.49	1.71	9.08**	3.17	3.68	5.13*
Other Issues						
School prayer	1.46	1.38	.72	3.13	3.33	.75
Environmental protection	1.50	1.50	.01	2.88	3.00	.20

Notes: For the Feminism Scale, high scores represent more feminist position. For the remaining statements, 1 = Strongly Agree; 2 = Agree; 3 = Disagree; 4 = Strongly Agree; all were coded for low scores to represent liberal responses.

*p < .05   **p < .01   ***p < .001

Source: Women's PAC Contributor Survey.

ATTITUDES ABOUT FEMINISM AND WOMEN'S RIGHTS

Feminist consciousness is more than the belief in women's equality with men, as we noted in Chapter 4; it also holds the patriarchal system responsible for women's inequality and oppression, and it advocates collective action to promote social change.[16] Both women and men can support feminist principles and hold feminist beliefs. Men can fully sympathize with feminist goals. But only women can feel a sense of personal identity with other women and with the limitations placed on women in a patriarchal society.[17] Feminist issues are more personally significant and more salient for women than they are for men. Because feminist issues are so salient to women, some contend, women tend to hold more extreme attitudes toward feminism, both favorable and unfavorable, than do men.[18] At the same time, the men who contribute serious money to these women's PACs comprise an exceptional—and exceptionally small—group of men who might have an exceptionally large commitment to feminist principles.

Among EMILY's List contributors, it is the women who are the most supportive of women's equality and feminism, reinforcing the argument that the personal salience of feminism to women increases the strength of their commitment. They express a higher sense of feminist consciousness, defined here as a combination of feminist self-identification and feelings toward the women's movement, than do the men who contribute to EMILY's List.[19] This difference between the women and men remains significant in a multivariate analysis controlling for ideology, strength of partisanship, and other social and economic variables.[20] EMILY's List women also are significantly more favorable than the men toward women's equality in business, industry, and government (see Table 5.1 on page 68). In fact, feminist consciousness and attitudes toward women's equality among EMILY's List men were found to be much closer to those of the women who contribute to the Republican WISH List.[21]

On other issues related to women's rights, however, there is no significant gender gap among the contributors to EMILY's List. The women and the men are nearly equal in their support for government help in improving women's situation, in their support for legal abortion, and in their disagreement that mothers with small children should remain at home rather than work outside the home.

The women and men who contribute to the Anthony List are very different in their attitudes from those who contribute to EMILY's List, but they are not very different from each other (see Table 5.1). There is no significant difference between Anthony List women and men on any of the issues related to feminism and women's rights, and their feminist consciousness is similarly low. Nor, within those narrow differences, are women consistently more liberal or more conservative on women's issues than are men; the women are slightly higher in feminist consciousness and more likely to support women's equality and government efforts to improve women's situation, but they also are slightly more opposed to legal abortion and to mothers with small children working outside the home.

In sum, the gender gap on feminist and women's rights issues is significant among the major contributors to EMILY's List, although it is somewhat narrow in size and in scope. And it is in the expected direction: Women display both higher feminist consciousness and greater support for women's equality. But the gender gap on women's rights issues is virtually nonexistent among the major contributors to the Anthony List.

ATTITUDES ABOUT EQUALITY

If the exceptional men who contribute serious money to women's PACS are not more feminist than the female contributors, perhaps they are driven by strong egalitarian values more generally. But the women and the men within each PAC hold similar views on several government policies to expand social and economic equality. The major contributors to EMILY's List and the Anthony List are very different from each other, regardless of gender, with those in EMILY's List expressing consistently more liberal views on equality issues than those in the Anthony List. This demonstrates the importance of partisanship and ideology, and the limited importance of gender, in the formulation of opinions toward government social welfare and antidiscrimination policies. At the same time, since women generally are more favorable toward such policies,[22] the fact that there is no gender gap among contributors to each of these PACs indicates that the men may actually be unusually egalitarian (see Table 5.1 on page 68.)

The only significant differences between the women and the men who contribute to EMILY's List, among the issues related to expanding equality, are in their attitudes toward government domestic spending in a general sense. The men are more conservative than the women, both more likely to support cutting domestic spending in order to reduce taxes and more likely to agree that the government is involved in things that people should do for themselves. Thus, while there is no gender gap among the women and men who contribute to EMILY's List regarding specific social welfare and antidiscrimination policies, there is a tendency for men to be more broadly opposed to widespread domestic programs that require higher taxes.

Among the major contributors to the Anthony List, there is no gender gap on any of the issues, either broad or specific, having to do with government efforts to expand social or economic equality. Both the women and the men are generally opposed to such efforts on the part of the government, reflecting their conservative ideology.

The men who contribute to each of these women's PACs are no more liberal than the women in their attitudes toward social welfare and antidiscrimination policies. But neither are they more conservative on these issues.

Thus, in a policy area—social and economic equality—where women are generally more liberal than men, both among the general public and among political elites, the absence of a gender gap among the women's PAC contributors may demonstrate an unusually high regard for equality among the men.

ATTITUDES ABOUT MILITARISM AND USE OF FORCE

Gender differences in preferences toward policies that deal with the use of force and violence have been found to be twice as great as differences regarding other policies. Issues of force and violence have been the issues that most divide women and men across time and when controlling for a variety of other influences.[23] Among women and men who are feminist sympathizers, furthermore, the gender gap in attitudes was found largely confined to issues of war and peace.[24] Concomitantly, it is on issues of militarism and the use of force that female and male contributors to both EMILY's List and the Anthony List diverge significantly. Although here again, the evidence of gender gaps within each PAC is mixed, it is stronger than in the other policy areas on which respondents expressed their views (see Table 5.1 on page 68).

The female contributors are more liberal, or more averse to the use of force, than are the male contributors on every issue, although the differences sometimes are very small. The female contributors to both EMILY's List and the Anthony List are more likely than their male counterparts to oppose the use of military force abroad, to oppose the death penalty, to oppose an increase in defense spending, and to favor a ban on handgun sales.

Among EMILY's List contributors, those differences are significant for two of the four issues: Women are less likely to support the use of military force and more likely to support a ban on handguns. Further, the difference between female and male EMILY's List contributors on these issues remains significant when other partisan, ideological, and socioeconomic variables are taken into account.[25]

Among the Anthony List contributors, the men are significantly more opposed than the women to handgun control, and the gender difference is larger than on any other issue. In addition, the issue with the second-largest difference between Anthony List female and male contributors is another use-of-force issue: capital punishment, which the women are more likely to oppose.

Finally, there is more evidence of gender difference regarding militarism and the use of force as a political priority. Respondents were asked to rate twelve issues on a one-to-five scale in terms of importance in deciding how to vote. Once again, the women and the men within each of the PACs are highly similar in their ratings of the issues. But in both EMILY's List and the Anthony List, the issue with the widest disparity between the female and the male contributors is the issue of national defense. The men in both PACs give the defense issue a higher rating than the women.

In sum, on issues related to force and violence, as in all other policy areas, the differences between the contributors to EMILY's List and to the Anthony List far outweigh the differences between the female and the male contributors within either PAC. But in each of the PACs, there is more evidence of a gender gap on use of force issues than in any other policy area.

POLICY PRIORITIES

Major contributors' policy priorities follow the same pattern as their policy preferences. The contributors to EMILY's List and the Anthony List are quite divergent in their priorities, while the women and men within each group are quite similar. Asked to name the most important problem facing the country, EMILY's List contributors emphasize domestic issues related to inequality and lack of public services, while Anthony List contributors emphasize the need for morality and public order. The major problems in the eyes of the women and the men who contribute to the Anthony List closely coincide. But for the women and the men who contribute to EMILY's List, there are a few differences demonstrating the particular weight that the men give to problems of inequality and issues of force or violence (see Table 5.2).

Among Anthony List donors, the overwhelming major problem for both women and men is the decline in moral or religious values, followed by opposition to legal abortion and the need for public order to reduce violent crime. Here it is the women, not the men, who are somewhat more likely to name violent crime as the major problem. But the top priorities of women and men are exactly the same.

The major problems cited by EMILY's List women and men are also similar. Education and economic inequality are the top-two problems, but women mention education most often while inequality tops the list for men. Health care is also a major concern for both the women and the men. But the men's frequent mentions of civil-rights issues illustrate their general egalitarianism, and their frequent mentions of violent crime and terrorist groups, well before the September 11, 2001, terrorist attacks on New York and Washington, D.C., illustrate their concern for problems related to force and violence. Conversely, the women's more frequent mentions of environmental problems may illustrate their concern for maintaining the quality of life.[26]

CONCLUSION

Politics in America is still mostly a man's world, but the presence of women in all aspects of politics is increasing steadily since the advent of the second-wave women's movement in the 1960s. While most political contributors still are men, especially among those who contribute $200 or more, most major

TABLE 5.2 THE MOST IMPORTANT PROBLEM FACING THIS COUNTRY AMONG
CONTRIBUTORS TO EMILY'S LIST AND SUSAN B. ANTHONY LIST (IN PERCENTAGES)

EMILY'S LIST			
WOMEN		MEN	
Education	17.9%	Economic inequality	13.1%
Economic inequality	14.3	Education	11.1
Environment	7.3	Health care	9.8
Health care	6.4	Crime/violence/public order	7.9
		Civil rights/racial problems	6.5
		National morale/unity	5.9
		Extremist groups/terrorists	4.6

SUSAN B. ANTHONY LIST			
WOMEN		MEN	
Moral/religious decay	46.2%	Moral/religious decay	50.0%
Abortion	11.5	Abortion	13.6
Crime/violence/public order	11.5	Crime/violence/public order	4.5

Note: Those problems receiving at least 4% of the mentions are listed in the table.
Source: Women's PAC Contributor Survey.

contributors to EMILY's List, The WISH List, and the Susan B. Anthony List
are women. We have examined the political preferences and priorities of the
female and the male contributors to EMILY's List and to the Anthony List,
the two PACs with a sufficient number of male donors, for comparison and
analysis. The gender gaps within each set of PAC contributors are small, even
nonexistent on most issues. But the gender gaps that do exist generally parallel those found in previous studies of both the general public and political
activists and elites.

There is no difference between the women and the men who contribute
to each PAC in their attitudes toward domestic policy issues dealing with social and economic equality, aside from a tendency for EMILY's List women to
express greater support than EMILY's List men for government domestic
spending at the expense of higher taxes. But EMILY's List women convey a
higher degree of feminist consciousness and support for gender equality than
its men. Furthermore, the men in both groups tend to be somewhat more supportive of the use of force, in their opposition to gun control and in their support and concern for national defense, military intervention, and fighting
violent crime.

In general, both the women and the men who contribute to EMILY's List
support women's political equality and oppose anti-abortion laws. But support

for these goals among EMILY's List women appears to be driven more by feminist consciousness, while that of the men appears to be driven more by general egalitarianism. Conversely, the support among Anthony List contributors for greater women's political equality and their opposition to abortion appear to be driven by social conservatism, tempered by the desire for women's leadership to reinforce their message. There is a minimal difference in the attitudes or priorities of the Anthony List women and men. The greatest disparities in attitudes are between the two women's PACs, not between the women and the men who support each PAC.

NOTES

1. Nancy Burns, Kay Lehman Schlozman, and Sidney Verba, *The Private Roots of Public Action: Gender, Equality, and Political Participation* (Cambridge, MA: Harvard University Press, 2001); Clifford W. Brown, Jr., Lynda W. Powell, and Clyde Wilcox, *Serious Money: Fundraising and Contributing in Presidential Nomination Campaigns* (New York: Cambridge University Press, 1995); Peter L. Francia, John C. Green, Paul S. Herrnson, Lynda W. Powell, and Clyde Wilcox, *The Financiers of Congressional Elections: Investors, Ideologues, and Intimates* (New York: Columbia University Press, 2003).

2. While the gender gap literature is voluminous, no one claims to explain completely the complex differences and similarities in attitudes between women and men. For examples, see Pamela Johnston Conover, "Feminists and the Gender Gap," *Journal of Politics* 50 (1988), pp. 985–1010; Pamela Johnston Conover and Virginia Sapiro, "Gender, Feminist Consciousness, and War," *American Journal of Political Science* 37 (1993), pp. 1079–1099; Elizabeth Adell Cook and Clyde Wilcox, "Feminism and the Gender Gap—A Second Look," *Journal of Politics* 53 (1991), pp. 1111–1122; Cynthia Dietch, "Sex Differences in Support for Government Spending," in *The Politics of the Gender Gap: The Social Construction of Political Influence*, ed. Carol M. Mueller (Newbury Park, CA: Sage, 1988); Susan E. Howell and Christine L. Day, "Complexities of the Gender Gap," *Journal of Politics* 62 (2000), pp. 858–874; Karen M. Kaufmann and John R. Petrocik, "The Changing Politics of American Men: Understanding the Sources of the Gender Gap," *American Journal of Political Science* 43 (1999), pp. 864–887; Mark Schlesinger and Caroline Heldman, "Gender Gap or Gender Gaps? New Perspectives on Support for Government Action and Policies," *Journal of Politics* 63 (2001), pp. 59–92; Richard Seltzer, Jody Newman, and Melissa Voorhees Leighton, *Sex as a Political Variable: Women as Candidates and Voters in American Elections* (Boulder, CO: Lynne Rienner, 1997); Robert Shapiro and Harpreet Majahan, "Gender Differences in Policy Preferences: A Summary of Trends from the 1960s to the 1980s," *Public Opinion Quarterly* 50 (1986), pp. 42–61.

3. See, for example, Susan J. Carroll, ed., *The Impact of Women in Public Office* (Bloomington, IN: Indiana University Press, 2001); Christine L. Day and Charles D. Hadley, "The Importance of Attitudes toward Women's Equality: Policy Preferences among Southern Party Elites," *Social Science Quarterly* 78 (1997), pp. 672–687; Anne E. Kelley, William E. Hulbary, and Lewis Bowman, "Gender, Party, and Political Ideology: The Case of Mid-Elite Party Activists in Florida," *Journal of Political Science* 17 (1989), pp. 6–18; Ruth B. Mandel and Debra L. Dodson "Do Women Officeholders Make a Difference?" in *The American Woman, 1992–1993: A Status Report*, ed. Paula Ries and Anne J. Stone (New York: W. W. Norton, 1992); Michele L. Swers, *The Difference Women Make: The Policy Impact of Women in Congress* (Chicago: University of Chicago Press, 2002); Sue Thomas, *How Women Legislate* (New York: Oxford University Press, 1994); Clyde Wilcox, Clifford W. Brown, Jr., and Lynda W. Powell, "Sex and the Political Contributor: The Gender Gap among Contributors to Presidential Candidates in 1988," *Political Research Quarterly* 46 (1993), pp. 355–369.

4. M. Kent Jennings and Barbara G. Farah, "Social Roles and Political Resources: An Over-Time Study of Men and Women in Party Elites," *American Journal of Political Science* 25 (1981), pp. 462–482; Jeane Kirkpatrick, *Political Woman* (New York: Basic Books, 1974); Jeane Kirkpatrick, *The New Presidential Elite: Men and Women in National Politics* (New York: Russell

Sage Foundation, 1976); Susan Gluck Mezey, "Does Sex Make a Difference? A Case Study of Women in Politics," *Western Political Quarterly* 31 (1978), pp. 492–501.

5. Mandel and Dodson, "Do Women Officeholders Make a Difference?"; Keith T. Poole and Harmon Zeigler, *Women, Public Opinion, and Politics* (New York: Longman, 1985); Susan Welch, "Are Women More Liberal Than Men in the U.S. Congress?" *Legislative Studies Quarterly* 10 (1985), pp. 125–134.

6. Beth Reingold, *Representing Women: Sex, Gender, and Legislative Behavior in Arizona and California* (Chapel Hill, NC: University of North Carolina Press, 2000); Karin L. Tamerius, "Sex, Gender, and Leadership in the Representation of Women," in *Gender Power, Leadership, and Governance,* ed. Georgia Duerst-Lahti and Rita Mae Kelly (Ann Arbor, MI: University of Michigan Press, 1995); Sue Thomas, *How Women Legislate;* Sue Thomas and Susan Welch, "The Impact of Gender on Activities and Priorities of State Legislators," *Western Political Quarterly* 44 (1991), pp. 445–456.

7. Rita Mae Kelly, Michelle A. Saint-Germain, and Jody D. Horn, "Female Public Officials: A Different Voice?" *Annals of the American Association of Political and Social Science* 515 (1991), pp. 77–87; Michele L. Swers, *The Difference Women Make.*

8. Day and Hadley "The Importance of Attitudes toward Women's Equality"; Kelley, Hulbary, and Bowman, "Gender, Party, and Political Ideology"; Ronald B. Rapoport, Walter J. Stone, and Alan I. Abramowitz, "Sex and the Caucus Participant: The Gender Gap and Presidential Nominations," *American Journal of Political Science* 34 (1990), pp. 725–740.

9. Wilcox, Brown, and Powell, "Sex and the Political Contributor."

10. Nancy Chodorow, *The Reproduction of Mothering: Psychoanalysis and the Sociology of Gender* (Berkeley, CA: University of California Press, 1978); Janet A. Flammang, *Women's Political Voice: How Women Are Transforming the Practice and Study of Politics* (Philadelphia, PA: Temple University Press, 1997); Carol Gilligan, *In a Different Voice: Psychological Theory and Women's Development* (Cambridge, MA: Harvard University Press, 1982).

11. Conover and Sapiro, "Gender, Feminist Consciousness, and War"; Howell and Day, "Complexities of the Gender Gap"; Shapiro and Mahajan, "Gender Differences in Policy Preferences"; Tom W. Smith, "The Polls: Gender and Attitudes toward Violence," *Public Opinion Quarterly* 48 (1984), pp. 384–396.

12. Rapoport, Stone, and Abramowitz, "Sex and the Caucus Participant"; Wilcox, Brown, and Powell, "Sex and the Political Contributor."

13. Conover, "Feminists and the Gender Gap."

14. Susan J. Carroll, "Women's Autonomy and the Gender Gap: 1980 and 1982," in *The Politics of the Gender Gap: The Social Construction of Political Influence,* ed. Carol M. Mueller (Newbury Park, CA: Sage, 1988).

15. Day and Hadley, "The Importance of Attitudes toward Women's Equality"; Wilcox, Brown, and Powell, "Sex and the Political Contributor."

16. Claire Knoche Fulenwider, *Feminism in American Politics: A Study of Ideological Influence* (New York: Praeger, 1980); Ethel Klein, *Gender Politics: From Consciousness to Mass Politics* (Cambridge, MA: Harvard University Press, 1984); Virginia Sapiro, *The Political Integration of Women: Role, Socialization, and Politics* (Urbana, IL: University of Illinois Press, 1983).

17. Cook and Wilcox, "Feminism and the Gender Gap"; Klein, *Gender Politics.*

18. Fulenwider, *Feminism in American Politics,* p. 77.

19. See Chapter 4, Note 8, for the operational definition of feminist consciousness used in this study.

20. Christine L. Day, Charles D. Hadley, and Megan Duffy Brown, "Gender, Feminism, and Partisanship among Women's PAC Contributors," *Social Science Quarterly* 82 (2001), pp. 687–700.

21. Ibid.

22. See the literature cited in Notes 2 and 3 of this chapter.

23. Howell and Day, "Complexities of the Gender Gap"; Shapiro and Mahajan, "Gender Differences in Policy Preferences"; Smith, "The Polls."

24. Cook and Wilcox, "Feminism and the Gender Gap."

25. Day, Hadley, and Brown, "Gender, Feminism, and Partisanship among Women's PAC Contributors."

26. See, for example, Tong's introduction to ecofeminism, a theoretical approach to feminism emphasizing humans' harmonious relationship with the natural world, in Rosemarie Putnam Tong, *Feminist Thought: A More Comprehensive Introduction,* 2nd ed. (Boulder, CO: Westview, 1998).

FEMALE CONTRIBUTORS AND FEMALE VOTERS

THE SAME VOICE?

Contributions from women's PACs including EMILY's List, The WISH List, and the Susan B. Anthony List have been vital to the success of many women's campaigns for public office. Electing women is no small feat in the United States, where the proportion of women in government is so small that it lags behind most industrialized and many less-developed countries. Women also continue to give fewer and smaller campaign contributions than men. In a country where campaign finance dominates electoral politics more than anywhere else, women's PACs work to close the gender gap both among campaign contributors and among elected officials.

Further, women's PACs do not just help to increase women's representation numerically; they also help to broaden women's representation ideologically. The diversity of women's PACs reflects the diversity of American women in their attitudes and in their partisan preferences, as each PAC supports different female candidates.

The major contributors to the three women's PACs surveyed for this study comprise a relatively small group who supply a large proportion of each PAC's money. A large majority of these major contributors, as we have seen, are women themselves. And they are politically active women who are generally wealthy, well educated, and confident in their ability to make a difference. To what extent do these women who give large amounts of money to the women's PACs represent the views of women in general? And to what extent do the women who contribute to the women's PACs represent the views of other female political contributors? In this chapter we compare the political attitudes and priorities of the female PAC contributors with the political attitudes and priorities of two other groups of women: (1) women in general; and (2) other women who have made political contributions to candidates, parties, or other candidate organizations.

The major concerns and priorities of all the groups of women—women's PAC contributors, other female contributors, and women in general—divide similarly along partisan lines, as do their political preferences. What sets the women's PAC contributors apart from the other groups of women is their high degree of polarization on the abortion issue and their high degree of polarization on other indicators of feminist or antifeminist consciousness. At the same time, however, the women who contribute to all three women's PACs are uniformly high in their support for women's equality with men in business, industry, and government. Thus, true to the women's PACs to which they contribute, the female donors are extremely divided in their attitudes toward abortion and feminism, but they are united in their support for greater gender equality among elected officials. It appears that the three women's PACs have effectively focused the efforts of wealthy female activists, channeling their activities and support toward electing more women who will advance their own, and their PAC's, respective political agendas.

DATA ON WOMEN AND OTHER FEMALE CONTRIBUTORS

We compare the political attitudes of women who contribute to women's PACs with those of women in the general public and with those of other female contributors, using the Women's PAC Contributor Survey and the American National Election Study (commonly known as the NES).[1]

Women make up a large majority of the contributors to the three women's PACs. In contrast, women make up only 41 percent of the other political contributors. The smaller proportion of women among political donors in general reflects previous findings that demonstrate the relatively greater activity of men in campaign finance.[2] Among women in the general public, Democrats outnumber Republicans by more than three to two (58 to 34 percent). The NES female political contributors are more evenly divided by party; 51 percent are Democrats and 42 percent are Republicans.

In comparing the female PAC contributors to general female contributors, it must be remembered that all of the female PAC contributors gave at least $200 in a single election cycle, while the self-reported contributions of the other female donors may be any amount; we cannot know how many exceed $200. Nevertheless, the differences between the women's PAC contributors and the other female contributors are often sufficiently large to be suggestive and to draw interesting, if tentative, conclusions about the differences among the various groups of women.[3]

POLITICAL ACTIVITY AND POLITICAL EFFICACY

The activism and affluence of the women's PAC contributors are extremely high, not only in comparison to women in general, but even in comparison to other female contributors. Fully 87 percent of the women's PAC contributors have family incomes exceeding $80,000; in contrast, only 4 percent of women in general, and only 31 percent of the NES female contributors, live in families earning at least $75,000.[4] The contrast in education level is equally stark: While over two-thirds of the women who contribute to the three women's PACs hold advanced degrees, this is true of only 8 percent of women in general and 24 percent of the NES female contributors.

Substantial majorities of female contributors to all three women's PACs disagree that "people like me don't have any say about what the government does," that "public officials [don't] care much about what people like me think," and that "sometimes politics and government seem so complicated that a person like me can't really understand what's going on." In contrast, women in general are fairly evenly divided on whether public officials care, and most do agree that people don't have a say and that politics and government are too complicated to understand. The NES female contributors, and especially the wealthiest among them (with incomes of at least $75,000), demonstrate a higher degree of political efficacy than women in general, as expected, but even they are less confident in their ability to influence policy than the female PAC contributors.

Such high levels of education and political efficacy among the women who contribute to women's PACs are reflected in their active political lives. Not only do the women's PAC contributors far surpass women in general in their political participation; they also outcampaign the general female contributors, even the wealthiest contributors, in all types of activities (see Table 6.1). Contributors to the women's PACs are nearly twice as likely as the NES female contributors to talk to others about the election; to display campaign buttons, bumper stickers, or signs; and to give money to political parties; they are more than twice as likely to attend candidate meetings or rallies or to do other party or candidate work. The female PAC donors' high participation levels are not explained by affluence alone. Among the NES female contributors, the highest-income group is in fact less likely than their lower-income counterparts to participate in the full range of political activities.

In sum, the women who contribute large amounts of money to the women's PACs are affluent activists, even relative to the small subset of women who contribute politically. And all contributors are more active, affluent, and politically efficacious than women in general. As we shall see, the contributors' attitudes also are more extreme than those of women in general, but the partisan divisions are similar across all the groups of women.

POLITICAL PRIORITIES

Two measures gauge the importance of particular issues in both surveys: questions about rating the importance of specific policy areas, and an open-ended question about the most important problem facing the country. Some issues, such as education, crime, and abortion, are high-priority issues for women in

TABLE 6.1   POLITICAL ACTIVITIES (IN PERCENTAGES)

	WOMEN'S PAC CONTRIBUTORS			WOMEN	NES FEMALE CONTRIBUTORS	NES FEMALE CONTRIBUTORS ≥ $75K INCOME
	EMILY	WISH	SBA			
Talked about candidates	79%	77%	85%	24%	45%	36%
Button/sticker/sign	53	47	73	10	33	30
Candidate meeting/rally	59	76	58	5	21	17
Other party/candidate work	39	48	42	3	12	9
Money to political party	62	39	58	5	47	44
Money to candidates	*	*	*	4	37	30
Money to political group	*	*	*	5	46	52
N	(140)	(79)	(26)	(893)	(83)	(23)

*By definition, contributors to the women's PACs have contributed to candidates and political groups.

Sources: Women's PAC Contributor Survey and 1996 NES.

both political parties. Other issues break down more along partisan lines, with Democratic women tending to emphasize inequality and social welfare issues, and Republican women emphasizing excessive government spending and the need for moral and public order.

The Women's PAC Contributor Survey asks respondents to rate the importance of twelve issues in deciding whether to support a candidate: abortion, tax policy, gender issues, health care, national defense, affirmative action, the environment, gay rights, jobs, race issues, AIDS, and trade policy. The NES survey asks respondents to rate the importance of four issues: abortion, defense spending, aid to blacks, and reduced government spending versus provision of services. Abortion is the issue of highest concern to women across the board. All groups of women—EMILY's List contributors, The WISH List contributors, Anthony List contributors, NES female contributors, and women in general—give the abortion issue the highest average rating of all the issues they are asked to rate. The difference lies in how many women within each group give the abortion issue the highest possible score on the five-point rating scale: 92 percent among Anthony List donors, 85 percent among EMILY's List donors, 63 percent among The WISH List donors, 50 percent among the NES female contributors, and 34 percent among women in general. There is virtually no difference between Republicans and Democrats in the latter two groups in their rating of the issue. Thus, abortion is an important issue for women generally, but not surprisingly, it is most crucial for the women who give substantial amounts of money to organizations that choose candidates based on their positions on the abortion issue.

Abortion, however, is mentioned only rarely by any of the women in any of these groups in answering the open-ended "most important problem" question. Here, the partisan divisions among the women's PAC contributors roughly parallel those among the NES female contributors as well as those among women in general. The primary concerns of The WISH List women, as usual, overlap those of both Democratic women and fellow Republican women.

Among Democratic women, education tops the list of concerns for both EMILY's List female contributors and Democratic female contributors in the NES survey; it is the third most important problem mentioned by Democratic women in general. Welfare is the second most important problem listed by Democratic women in general, and issues related to social welfare and inequality also dominate the remaining top concerns of both Democratic contributor groups: Economic inequality and health care are the next two top concerns for EMILY's List women, and welfare, unemployment, poverty, and inequality follow education as top concerns for the Democratic female contributors. Among Democratic women in general, however, violent crime is the number one concern for the largest number, and it is a major concern shared by many of the Republican women.

Among Republican women, moral or religious decay tops the list of concerns for both Anthony List female contributors and Republican female contributors in the NES survey; it is also third on the list for Republican women in general. Violent crime also is one of the top three most important problems listed by Anthony List female contributors (problem number three), Republican female contributors (problem number three), and Republican women in general (problem number two). Legalized abortion is the second most frequently mentioned problem among the Anthony List women. Republican women also emphasize the problem of too much government spending; it is the most frequently mentioned problem among Republican women in general, and the second most frequently mentioned problem among Republican female contributors.

For The WISH List women, education is the most important problem, and health care is fourth on their list; they share these concerns primarily with the Democratic women. But moral or religious decay is second on their list of important problems, a concern they share mostly with the other Republican women. At the same time, the third most frequently mentioned problem among WISH List female donors is excessive influence of religion in politics, suggesting that there may be some disagreement within The WISH List over how strong a role religious morality should play in making public policy. In general, the issues cited by WISH List women as the country's most important problems overlap those of both Democratic and other Republican women.

The female contributors to the three women's PACs differ from the other groups of women primarily in the overwhelming number who rate the abortion issue of highest importance. But the issue also is rated highly, relative to other issues, by other female contributors and by women in general regardless of political party. The major political concerns listed by all groups of women overlap to a considerable extent, with divisions occurring along partisan lines, and with the pro-choice Republican WISH List donors serving as something of a moderate force by giving high priority to issues mentioned often by activists in both parties. The concerns of female activists are not out of line with the concerns of women in general. Thus, a political agenda driven by female campaign contributors also addresses many of the primary concerns of women in the general public.

ATTITUDES RELATED TO FEMINISM AND WOMEN'S EQUALITY

The women who contribute to EMILY's List, The WISH List, and the Anthony List are considerably more polarized on attitudes related to feminism than are the NES female contributors who consider themselves Democrats and Republicans. Female contributors are, in turn, more polarized on feminist issues than are female Democrats and Republicans in general. Furthermore, the polarization among the women's PAC contributors does not break down neatly along partisan lines. Instead, contributors to the Republican pro-choice WISH List resemble EMILY's List contributors and other Democratic female contributors on most feminist issues, while distancing themselves from contributors to the pro-Republican Anthony List and other Republican female contributors. Thus, the women's PAC contributors lie at opposite extremes of the feminist divide. The exception to this pattern is the consensus on women's equality with men in business, industry, and government. Strong support for gender equality unites the otherwise contentious female contributors to all three women's PACs.

The increasing polarization of the two major political parties around feminist issues and abortion is evident to some extent in the attitudes of women in general and female contributors,[5] and it is even more evident in the highly polarized attitudes of contributors to the pro-choice Democratic EMILY's List and to the pro-life Republican Anthony List. But the pro-choice Republican WISH List donors do not fit the pattern. Instead, the laissez-faire conservatives of The WISH List, more aligned with the fiscally conservative wing than with the religious moralistic wing of the Republican party, tend to be strongly supportive of free market and property rights and opposed to a large governmental role in social welfare and economic regulation.[6] Their emphasis on individualism and personal privacy makes them generally sympathetic to many feminist goals, including reproductive freedom and women's freedom to pursue nontraditional roles and careers, despite their aversion to much of the Democratic domestic agenda.

We examine four different indicators of sympathy or antipathy toward feminism: attitudes toward women's equality, attitudes toward abortion, attitudes toward mothers with small children working outside the home, and feelings about the women's movement.[7]

Women's equality with men in business, industry, and government is the issue with the smallest variation across groups of women (see Table 6.2). Substantial majorities of women in every PAC and partisan group agree that women and men should have equal roles. Still, Democratic female voters are more likely than Republican female voters to support women's equality (80 versus 72 percent). Among the NES female contributors, Democrats and Republicans are even further apart on the issue of women's equality (91 versus 63 percent). This concurs with numerous studies showing that the mass public tends to be less polarized along partisan lines generally than do partisan activists and elites.[8] But the women's PAC donors are not polarized on this issue. Anthony List contributors, despite their antifeminist leanings on the other indicators, are not far from contributors to the other two women's PACs in their support for women's equality. Fully 87 percent of Anthony List female contributors support women's equality in business, industry, and government, compared to 97 percent agreement in The WISH List and perfect 100 percent agreement in EMILY's List. This near-congruity with the two pro-choice groups on women's equality evidently reflects the Anthony List's overt support for women in at least one nontraditional role: that of high-level state and national elective office.

TABLE 6.2 ATTITUDES RELATED TO FEMINISM AND WOMEN'S EQUALITY

	WOMEN'S PAC CONTRIBUTORS			WOMEN		NES FEMALE CONTRIBUTORS		NES FEMALE CONTRIBUTORS ≥ $75K INCOME
	EMILY	WISH	ANTHONY	DEM.	REP.	DEM.	REP.	
Women/men equal roles								
Strongest agreement[a]	75%	61%	25%	62%	40%	81%	26%	71%
Agree[b]	100	97	87	80	72	91	63	92
Disagree[c]	0	3	13	9	15	5	14	4
Women's movement								
Mean relative feeling thermometer	.46	.36	−.63	.19	−.02	.29	−.22	.11
Mothers with small children stay at home								
Agree[d]	6%	13%	80%	42%	52%	22%	56%	26%
Disagree[e]	94	87	20	42	32	54	27	52
Abortions should always be personal choice								
Agree	91%	87%	0%	51%	37%	71%	28%	65%
N	(140)	(79)	(26)	(516)	(299)	(42)	(35)	(23)

Notes: Entries are in percentages except for the mean relative feeling thermometer scores.
See Appendix C for question wording.
[a]PAC surveys: 1 on 4-point scale; NES: 1 on 7-point scale.
[b]PAC surveys: 1 and 2 on 4-point scale; NES: 1, 2, and 3 on 7-point scale.
[c]PAC surveys: 3 and 4 on 4-point scale; NES: 5, 6, and 7 on 7-point scale.
[d]PAC surveys: 1 and 2 on 4-point scale; NES: 1 and 2 on 5-point scale.
[e]PAC surveys: 3 and 4 on 4-point scale; NES: 4 and 5 on 5-point scale.
Sources: Women's PAC Contributor Survey and 1996 NES.

When it comes to assessing the women's movement, however, Anthony List contributors demonstrate by far the strongest antipathy to the movement. We calculate relative feeling thermometer scores to gauge respondents' feelings about the women's movement.[9] At the two extremes in their feelings toward the women's movement are the pro-choice Democratic EMILY's List contributors with a mean score of .46 and the pro-life Republican Anthony List contributors with a mean score of −.63. Close to EMILY's List contributors with their endorsement of the women's movement are the pro-choice Republican WISH List contributors with a mean score of .36. Also polarized, but less so than the women's PAC donors, are Democratic and Republican female contributors with respective mean scores of .29 and −.22. Finally, Democratic and Republican women in general, with respective mean scores of .19 and −.02, reflect their partisan differences, but they are much closer together than are the activist partisan groups.

The same pattern—with the pro-choice and pro-life women's PAC contributors demonstrating the highest degree of polarization, the NES female contributors demonstrating the second-highest degree of polarization, and women in general demonstrating the most moderate views—emerges in response to questions about whether mothers with small children should stay at home and whether abortion should be legal. Female contributors to both EMILY's List (94 percent) and The WISH List (87 percent) are nearly unanimous in their disagreement that "mothers should remain at home with young children and not work" in contrast with only 20 percent of Anthony List contributors. Just over half (54 percent) of Democratic female contributors disagree that mothers should stay at home in contrast to only a quarter (27 percent) of Republican female contributors. Among women in general, only ten percentage points separate Republicans from Democrats who feel that a woman's place is in the home—at least if she has small children.

On the abortion issue, once again the women's PAC contributors are extremely polarized with 91 percent of EMILY's List contributors and 87 percent of The WISH List contributors expressing the strongest support for freedom of individual choice and with all 100 percent of the Anthony List contributors expressing the strongest support for laws prohibiting abortion. The NES female contributors also are quite polarized along partisan lines on the abortion issue although less so than those who contribute to women's PACs: 71 percent of Democratic female contributors, but only 28 percent of Republican female contributors, agree that "by law a woman should be able to obtain an abortion as a matter of personal choice." Women in general are not quite as divided along partisan lines: 51 percent of Democratic women and 37 percent of Republican women agree that abortion should always be a matter of personal choice.

Are the affluent, activist women who contribute large amounts of money to EMILY's List, The WISH List, and the Anthony List and who are so highly opinionated on feminist issues, representative of affluent female contributors generally? The right-hand column of Table 6.2 on page 83 displays the feminist-related attitudes of the wealthiest group of general female contributors, those with annual family incomes of $75,000 or more. While their numbers in the NES survey are small for drawing conclusions (and too small to further subdivide by party), the numbers are still suggestive. Although the partisan distribution of the wealthiest group of female contributors is very similar to the partisan distribution of female contributors generally—if anything, the wealthy donors are slightly more Republican—the wealthy group of contributors is relatively feminist in their attitudes toward women's equality, the women's movement, working mothers, and legalized abortion. Women of higher socioeconomic status tend to be more open to feminist ideas than lower-status women, perhaps because higher-status women are more likely to be in male-dominated positions where they are subject to feelings of relative deprivation.[10]

In sum, female contributors to EMILY's List, The WISH List, and the Anthony List, aside from their common belief that women and men should have equal roles in government and the private sector, are extremely divided in their attitudes toward feminism, working mothers, and legalized abortion with EMILY's List and The WISH List contributors at the feminist extreme and Anthony List contributors at the antifeminist extreme. Not only are these PAC contributors much more polarized on feminist issues than women in general, they are even more polarized than other active Democratic and Republican female contributors. The three women's PACs seem to appeal to highly specialized groups of female activists, women unusual not only in their financial commitment to electoral politics but also in their strength of support for, or opposition to, key aspects of feminist ideology.

OTHER POLITICAL ISSUES

The pattern we observed in attitudes related to feminism—with EMILY's List and Anthony List donors generally the most polarized, followed by other female contributors and then by women in general—emerges once again in responses to questions about ideological self-identification, but the pattern does not necessarily hold across other types of issues. In this section we examine the attitudes of the various groups of women on a variety of other political issues included in both surveys to see whether the same patterns of support and opposition, relative unity and polarization, emerge across different policy areas. What we find is that sometimes they do and sometimes they do not. Nor is there a clear pattern across policy types, such as social welfare, racial, or social/moral issues (see Table 6.3 on page 86).

What we do find, similar to the feminist-related issues, is that women in general, once again, are less polarized along partisan lines; their attitudes on all the issues lie between the extremes of the activist female contributor groups.

TABLE 6.3   OTHER ISSUE ATTITUDES (IN PERCENTAGES)

	WOMEN'S PAC CONTRIBUTORS			NES FEMALE CONTRIBUTORS	
	EMILY	WISH	SBA	DEM.	REP.
Government Taxing/Spending					
Support cuts	1%	37%	62%	7%	39%
Oppose cuts	99	63	38	93	61
Defense Spending					
Support increase	9%	60%	71%	16%	70%
Oppose increase	91	40	29	63	15
Handgun Sales					
Support ban	86%	65%	17%	78%	47%
Oppose ban	14	35	83	22	53
Affirmative Action for Blacks					
Support	58%	13%	4%	41%	9%
Oppose	42	87	96	48	89
Aid to Blacks					
Support	96%	66%	38%	47%	9%
Oppose	5	34	63	24	70
Government Health Insurance					
Support	95%	46%	42%	50%	15%
Oppose	5	54	58	23	71
School Prayer					
Oppose	90%	57%	17%	36%	6%
Death Penalty for Murder					
Support	34%	92%	36%	54%	86%
Oppose	66	8	64	46	14
Protect Gays from Discrimination					
Support	95%	75%	18%	95%	30%
Oppose	5	25	82	5	70
Jobs/Good Standard of Living					
Support	54%	10%	13%	48%	6%
Oppose	46	90	87	31	81
N	(140)	(79)	(26)	(42)	(35)

Notes: All questions in the Women's PAC surveys are set to a 1–4 scale. In the NES survey, all questions are set to 1–7 scales except for government taxing/spending, handgun sales, affirmative action, death penalty for murder, and protection of gays, all of which are on 1–2 scales with a third category of volunteered answers for affirmative action and school prayer.

See Appendix C for question wording.

Sources: Women's PAC Contributor Survey and 1996 NES.

Nor are the wealthiest contributors significantly different in their attitudes from the rest of the NES female contributors on the issues discussed in this section. Therefore, we confine our analysis to the following groups of female contributors: the contributors to EMILY's List, The WISH List, and the Anthony List, and the Democratic and Republican female contributors in the NES survey.

Again, female contributors to EMILY's List anchor the left end of the ideological spectrum: They are the most liberal group of contributors on every issue just as they were on feminist-related issues. But rather than being consistently more moderate than EMILY's List contributors, the Democratic female contributors in the NES survey are nearly indistinguishable from the EMILY's List contributors in their extreme views on two issues: opposition to cuts in government spending and taxing and support for government protection from discrimination for homosexuals.

Once again, female contributors to the Anthony List anchor the right end of the ideological spectrum: They are the most conservative group of contributors on the majority of issues. But the Republican female contributors in the NES survey are not consistently more moderate than the Anthony List contributors. In fact the Republican female contributors are highly similar to the Anthony List contributors on three issues—defense spending, affirmative action, and government provision of jobs and a good standard of living—and they are even more conservative than the Anthony List contributors on four more issues: aid to blacks, government health insurance, school prayer, and the death penalty.

The WISH List contributors, although generally as liberal as EMILY's List contributors on feminist issues, are much more conservative than EMILY's List contributors on the issues in Table 6.3 on page 86. More than half of The WISH List contributors call themselves ideological moderates, and indeed, their attitudes lie between the extremes of EMILY's List and Anthony List contributors on most of the issues. On two issues—government health insurance and government provision of jobs and a good standard of living—The WISH List contributors are virtually as conservative as the Anthony List donors, congruent with their laissez-faire conservative ideology. The WISH List donors are even the most conservative of all contributor groups on use of the death penalty for murder.

The death penalty issue is the outlier among issues: While the generally moderate WISH List donors are hard-line conservatives, EMILY's List and Anthony List contributors are liberal allies, with two-thirds of each group opposing capital punishment. While the Anthony List donors' opposition to the death penalty is out of step with their conservative ideology, it may reflect the religious beliefs of many members. More than half of the Anthony List contributors are Roman Catholic, far more than in any other contributor group, and in a multivariate analysis of PAC contributors' policy preferences, Catholicism was the only significant variable explaining death penalty attitudes.[11]

The consistently high degree of polarization on feminist issues between the female contributors to EMILY's List and to The WISH List on the one hand, and the female contributors to the Anthony List on the other, does not carry over to all other types of issues. The WISH List contributors, closely allied with EMILY's List contributors on feminist issues, part company with EMILY's List contributors in a conservative direction on most other policies. Furthermore, the NES female contributors, divided along partisan lines, are as extreme in their attitudes—or even more so—as the women's PAC contributors in many of their policy preferences.

CONCLUSION

The women who make large contributions to EMILY's List, The WISH List, and the Susan B. Anthony List are generally active and well connected in the world of electoral politics and campaign finance. Their levels of education, political efficacy, and political involvement are even higher than those of other female political contributors, and they are much higher than those of women in general. Their commitment to their cause—pro-life or pro-choice, feminist or antifeminist, as the case may be—appears to be strong and consistent relative both to their attitudes on other types of issues and to other female political contributors. The hope of PAC leaders, of course, is that such strong commitment may translate into influence over election results, and ultimately over policy.

The importance of the three women's PACs, then, is to channel financial contributions of a small number of affluent, politically active women in a particular direction: toward female candidates who are Democratic and pro-choice in the case of EMILY's List, Republican and pro-choice in the case of The WISH List, and pro-life (and generally Republican) in the case of the Anthony List. Despite the relatively extreme polarization around issues of feminism and abortion among the women who contribute to the women's PACs, their political attitudes are not out of line with other women affiliated with their respective political parties. Furthermore, their strong and unified support for greater gender equality in positions of political leadership help provide better representation for women across the ideological spectrum.

NOTES

1. The data on women in general, and on the subset of women who reported making contributions to candidates, political parties, and/or other groups that support or oppose candidates, come from the 1996 American National Election Study (NES), which biennially surveys a sample of U.S. voting-age adults. The total number of female respondents in the NES survey is 893, and the total number of women who said they contributed to candidates, political parties, or other candidate groups is 83, representing about 9 percent of total female respondents. Unanswered questions in both our survey and in the NES survey are treated as missing data unless indicated otherwise. See Chapter 3, Note 12, for the full NES citation.

2. Nancy Burns, Kay Lehman Schlozman, and Sidney Verba, *The Private Roots of Public Action: Gender, Equality, and Political Participation* (Cambridge, MA: Harvard University Press, 2001); Sidney Verba, Kay Lehman Schlozman, and Henry E. Brady, *Voice and Equality: Civic Voluntarism in American Politics* (Cambridge, MA: Harvard University Press, 1995); Clifford W. Brown, Jr., Lynda W. Powell, and Clyde Wilcox, *Serious Money: Fundraising and Contributing in Presidential Nomination Campaigns* (New York: Cambridge University Press, 1995); Peter L. Francia, John C. Green, Paul S. Herrnson, Lynda W. Powell, and Clyde Wilcox, *The Financiers of Congressional Elections: Investors, Ideologues, and Intimates* (New York: Columbia University Press, 2003); Larry Makinson and the staff of the Center for Responsive Politics, *The Big Picture: The Money behind the 2000 Elections* (Washington, D.C.: Center for Responsive Politics, 2001).

3. See Appendix C for the exact wording of questions used from the NES survey. The NES is generally conducted every two years, or every national election year. However, we chose the 1996 NES survey over the 1998 and 2000 surveys for comparison because the 1996 survey contains many more questions on political issues that are comparable to the questions in the Women's PAC Contributor Survey. Many of the comparisons between the female contributors to the three women's PACs on the one hand, and the women and female contributors from the NES survey on the other hand, are based on questions that are worded somewhat differently, and the surveys were conducted in different years; therefore, direct comparisons should be examined with caution, and tests of significance are inappropriate.

4. The income comparisons are not direct because the Women's PAC Contributor Survey and the NES used different cutoff points in questions about family income.

5. Greg D. Adams, "Abortion: Evidence of an Issue Evolution," *American Journal of Political Science* 41 (1997), pp. 718–737; Jo Freeman, "Change and Continuity for Women at the Republican and Democratic National Conventions," *American Review of Politics* 18 (1997), pp. 353–368; Christina Wolbrecht, *The Politics of Women's Rights: Parties, Positions, and Change* (Princeton, NJ: Princeton University Press, 2000); Lisa Young, *Feminists and Party Politics* (Ann Arbor, MI: University of Michigan Press, 2000).

6. Rebecca Klatch, *Women of the New Right* (Philadelphia, PA: Temple University Press, 1987).

7. Both the Women's PAC Contributor Survey and the NES survey contain identical or very similar items on these four indicators.

8. David King, "The Polarization of American Parties and Mistrust of Government," in *Why People Don't Trust Government,* ed. Joseph Nye, Philip Zelikow, and David King (Cambridge, MA: Harvard University Press, 1997); Paul Dimaggio, John Evans, and Bethany Bryson, "Have Americans' Social Attitudes Become More Polarized?" *American Journal of Sociology* 102 (1996), pp. 690–755; Herbert Weisberg, Audrey Haynes, and Jon Krosnick, "Social Group Polarization in 1992," in *Democracy's Feast: Elections in America,* ed. Herbert Weisberg (Chatham, NJ: Chatham House, 1995); Benjamin I. Page and Robert Y. Shapiro, *The Rational Public* (Chicago: University of Chicago Press, 1992); Alan Abramowitz, "Viability, Electability, and Candidate Choice in a Presidential Primary Election: A Test of Competing Models," *Journal of Politics* 51 (1989), pp. 977–992; James McCann, "Presidential Nomination Activists and Political Representation: A View from the Active Minority Studies," in *In Pursuit of the White House: How We Choose Our Presidential Nominees,* ed. William Mayer (Chatham, NJ: Chatham House, 1996); Nelson W. Polsby and Aaron Wildavsky, *Presidential Elections: Strategies and Structures of American Politics,* 9th ed. (Chatham, NJ: Chatham House, 1996); Lawrence R. Jacobs and Robert Y. Shapiro, *Politicians Don't Pander: Political Manipulation and the Loss of Democratic Responsiveness* (Chicago: University of Chicago Press, 2000).

9. For information on calculating the relative feeling thermometer scores, see Chapter 4, Note 8. Mean feeling thermometer scores are based on feelings toward the following groups, in addition to the women's movement, that were included in both the Women's PAC Contributor Survey and the NES survey: environmentalists, conservatives, liberals, unions, big business, people on welfare, the elderly, fundamentalists, blacks, whites, gays, the military, and the federal government.

10. Keith T. Poole and Harmon Zeigler, *Women, Public Opinion, and Politics* (New York: Longman, 1985).

11. Christine L. Day and Charles D. Hadley, "Electing Women to National Public Office: Partisanship and Ideology in Women's PACs," presented at the annual meeting of the American Political Science Association, September, 2001, San Francisco, CA.

CONCLUSION

Women's PACs have helped to expand the presence of women in Congress, in governors' mansions, and in other elective offices at all levels of government since the mid-1970s. EMILY's List, The WISH List, and the Susan B. Anthony List represent the partisan and ideological diversity of the PACs that raise money primarily or exclusively for female candidates. EMILY's List attained superstar status in the PAC universe within a few years of its 1986 founding, helping to elect pro-choice Democratic women. The WISH List and the Susan B. Anthony List, founded in the early 1990s, raised money on a smaller scale, and they respectively have helped to elect Republican pro-choice women and pro-life women.

Major donors to these three women's PACs—donors who contribute at least $200 in a single election cycle—participate actively in electoral politics beyond giving money to women's PACs; their activity levels surpass even those of other high-income women who contribute to political parties, candidates, or other groups. They are relatively wealthy and privileged like most major political contributors. But while political contributors generally are predominantly men, at least 90 percent of the contributors to EMILY's List and The WISH List, and over half of the contributors to the Anthony List, are women. Thus the three PACs have successfully channeled the contributions of affluent activists toward female candidates with specific partisan affiliations and specific positions on the abortion issue. By promoting women's representation in government, they appeal mostly to female contributors.

The political attitudes of the women's PAC contributors vary widely across the ideological landscape, reflecting the differences among the three PACs themselves. The attitudes of EMILY's List contributors are largely consistent with liberal feminist ideology, favoring active government involvement in preventing discrimination and providing social services, but opposing laws prohibiting abortion or imposing other traditional or religious moral values. The attitudes of The WISH List contributors, while also supporting legalized abortion, reflect a laissez-faire conservative ideology, favoring little government intervention in domestic affairs and supporting a strong national defense. The attitudes of Anthony List contributors largely reflect a socially conservative ideology that, in many ways, is the antithesis of liberal feminism: opposed to a strong welfare state, but favorable toward general government endorsement of traditional and religious values including the prohibition of abortion.

The issue that unites the major contributors to all three women's PACs is the issue of gender equality. The high degree of support across all three donor groups for women's equality with men in business, industry, and government coincides with the mission of the three PACs to increase women's representation in government.

SUMMARY AND OVERVIEW

Women's PACs are both a product of and a reaction to the second wave of the women's rights movement that began in the mid-1960s. Women's rights activists began emphasizing electoral politics as a strategy for achieving feminist goals in the early- to mid-1970s, having at first shunned electoral politics as a linchpin of the patriarchal establishment. The first organizations emphasizing the election of women were largely nonpartisan, and such issues as women's equality and abortion in the 1970s cut across partisan lines, with supporters and opponents in each political party. By the time EMILY's List, The WISH List, and the Anthony List were founded in the mid-1980s to early 1990s, the two major political parties were polarized on issues related to gender roles and reproductive rights. Feminists had become a key constituency of the Democratic party as that party became identified with a broader civil rights agenda. Antifeminists of the Christian Right became a key constituency of the Republican party as that party became increasingly identified with traditional moral and religious values.

Thus, the decision by the founders of EMILY's List to align their PAC overtly with the Democratic party was consistent with the Democrats' official pro-choice position on the abortion issue. The decision by the founders of The WISH List, six years later, to establish a PAC for Republican pro-choice female candidates may have put the organization at odds with the official pro-life stance of the Republican party, but it reflected their preference for the broader Republican antigovernment and probusiness agenda. Finally, as women's presence in government grew and female elected officials became increasingly accepted, not only by feminists but also by antifeminists, many pro-life activists decided they should have their own spokeswomen in government, resulting in the founding of the Anthony List.

All three organizations, then, are at odds with each other over their policy positions. The biggest rift among them, however, is over the abortion issue. Thus, EMILY's List and The WISH List, while always supporting different candidates, do feel some mutual affinity and their leaders meet together on occasion, while the two pro-choice groups and the Anthony List remain adamantly opposed to each other. In fact, the Anthony List, with its policy of supporting pro-life men who run against pro-choice women, has contributed to the campaigns of men running against female candidates supported by EMILY's List and The WISH List.

All three women's PACs attribute most of their fund-raising success to the process of bundling individual contributions in addition to making direct PAC contributions to candidates. Bundling enables the PACs to channel more money to their chosen candidates than they could legally through direct PAC contributions alone. Thus, in electoral campaigns generally dominated by male incumbents, women's PACs have celebrated the success of many female open-seat candidates and even some challengers in addition to an increasing number of female incumbents. Having excelled at raising money for female candidates running for Congress and statewide office, the three women's PACs increased their operations during the last decade, adding more services for candidates such as issue research and training, and expanding their activities to state and local elections.

The contributors of $200 or more are a tiny percentage of each PAC's donor pool, but they contribute more than a third overall of the PACs' receipts. Most of the major donors in all three groups have postgraduate degrees and high-status professional or managerial jobs, earning more than $80,000 per year. Their high levels of political activity reflect the extraordinary amount of confidence they have in their ability to influence policy through their participation. Although the large number of women among them makes these groups of donors unusual among major political contributors, it conforms with previous findings that women, more than men, are driven to participate politically by their views on the abortion issue, and they are more interested and engaged when women are on the ballot.

All three women's PACs recruit contributors through personal networks and direct mail, and two of them, EMILY's List and the Anthony List, rely primarily on direct mail. But the perception among the largest number of contributors to all three PACs, especially among the female contributors, is that they became interested in contributing to their respective PACs through contacts with friends and acquaintances. Apparently, personal networking among activists sparks the interest in contributing even when organization leaders believe that most donors are responding to direct-mail solicitations. Once they begin to contribute, habitual donors tend to increase the amounts they give over time.

Personal networking between donor groups may be facilitated by the fact that large numbers of contributors to all three women's PACs are involved in business and professional organizations, in civic and community groups, in educational and cultural organizations, and in service organizations. On the other hand, EMILY's List donors are much more likely to participate in women's rights organizations while Anthony List donors are much more involved in religious organizations, differences that reflect their political and ideological disparities. No amount of personal interaction is likely to bridge the divide in political attitudes and priorities evident in contributors' survey responses.

The WISH List donors perhaps would be the most open to any kind of political alliance with either of the other two donor groups, being generally the most moderate of the three. More than half of The WISH List contributors see themselves as moderates, in contrast to the overwhelming majority of EMILY's List and Anthony List contributors who refer to themselves respectively as liberals and conservatives. The political priorities of The WISH List donors overlap those of both of the other women's PACs. With EMILY's List donors they share a deep interest in improved education and legalized abortion; with Anthony List donors they share a deep concern over high taxes, moral decay, and the need for public order.

The WISH List donors also are the most ambivalent about their partisanship, being much more likely to call themselves independents or weak partisans than either the overwhelmingly Democratic EMILY's List donors or the overwhelmingly Republican Anthony List donors. On the surface it may seem odd that contributors to the overtly Republican WISH List would be less partisan than the nominally nonpartisan Anthony List. But the partisan ambivalence of The WISH List donors is less surprising given the PAC's pro-choice position on the abortion issue, which is contrary to the official position of the national Republican party.

The relative moderation of The WISH List donors thus places them ideologically between the other two donor groups. Nevertheless, any alliance between The WISH List donors and the donors to either of the other two PACs would be, at best, an uneasy one. In their ideology and in their partisanship, The WISH List donors are closer to Anthony List donors: more conservative than liberal, and more Republican than Democratic. But their degree of feminist consciousness is much closer to that of EMILY's List donors than to that of the largely antifeminist Anthony List donors.

The policy preferences of The WISH List donors lie between the more liberal preferences of EMILY's List donors and the more conservative preferences of Anthony List donors on fifteen out of seventeen specific issues in the Women's PAC Contributor Survey. But the laissez-faire conservative contributors to The WISH List are closer to the liberal feminist contributors to EMILY's List in their opinions on such social issues as abortion, women's equality, school prayer, gay rights, and handgun control. And they are closer to the socially conservative contributors to the Anthony List in their opposition to government provision of jobs or health care and to affirmative action, as well as in their support for a stronger national defense. Further, The WISH List donors are the most extreme on two of the seventeen issues: They are the most supportive of both imposing capital punishment for murder and using military force abroad. In general, the laissez-faire conservatism of The WISH List donors is comfortable with neither the liberal feminism of EMILY's List donors nor the social conservatism of Anthony List donors.

The internal divisions among each group of PAC contributors are both smaller and fewer than the divisions between them. This includes the differences in attitudes between the women and the men within each donor group, which are minimal. It is interesting, however, that the gender gaps that do appear among the contributors to EMILY's List and among the contributors to the Anthony List parallel some of the attitudinal gender gaps found in other studies of political activists and elites. The men in both groups are somewhat more likely than the women to support the use of military force abroad and, among EMILY's List contributors, the men are more opposed to handgun control. In addition, the feminist consciousness among EMILY's List women is significantly higher than that of EMILY's List men, whose support for EMILY's List apparently derives from a more general commitment to egalitarianism.

Still, it is the attitudes related to feminism that tend to unite contributors within PACs the most and to divide contributors between PACs the most, with EMILY's List and WISH List donors on one side of the feminist divide and Anthony List donors on the other. Despite their different partisan affinities, contributors to EMILY's List and to The WISH List are strongly united in their support for the women's movement, for legalized abortion, and for mothers with small children being able to work outside the home. Anthony List contributors, in contrast, oppose legalized abortion, express negative feelings about the women's movement, and feel that mothers with small children should stay at home. The women who contribute to the three women's PACs, compared to other female political contributors and to women in general, are particularly polarized on these issues related to women's rights and gender roles.

At the same time, the women who contribute to all three women's PACs, compared to other female political contributors and to women in general, are more inclined to agree that women and men should have equal roles in business, industry, and government. It is true that Anthony List female contributors are somewhat less enthusiastic about gender equality than the other two women's PAC donor groups. But even Anthony List female contributors, so negative toward other aspects of feminism, are far more likely than other Republican female political contributors, and women in general of either party, to support women's equality with men.

This exceptional support for gender equality in business, industry, and government across all three women's PAC donor groups has generated significant contributions in support of female candidates across the partisan and ideological spectrum. The result is not only greater representation of women in government, but also greater representation of the *diversity* of women in government.

IMPLICATIONS: WOMEN IN GOVERNMENT

Divided as they are on fundamental questions about the role of government, EMILY's List, The WISH List, and the Anthony List collectively have enhanced the representation of women in elective office. This has more than just symbolic effect. Women do make a difference in the political agenda and in the governmental process. Systematically excluding particular groups from positions of power damages the legitimacy of a democratic government and wastes the talents and energies of entire segments of society. Furthermore, women enter into politics with different life experiences and different gender role expectations from those of men; they are more likely to have had hands-on experience with caregiving and other domestic responsibilities; they are, by definition, rebelling against the status quo by running for office whether or not they subscribe to feminist goals. These differences are manifest in the way women and men govern.

Women, like men, are diverse in their preferences and priorities, but collectively they have altered the government agenda. Female legislators tend to be more active and involved than men on women's, children's, and family issues ranging from education and health care to employment discrimination and domestic violence.[1] Women are more likely than their male legislative colleagues to perceive women as a key constituency and to express commitment to representing women's concerns.[2] Women of both political parties also tend to display more liberal roll-call voting patterns than their male partisan colleagues on a variety of issues.[3]

Studies show that these gender differences increase as women gain a stronger presence in government. Critical mass theory suggests that when women reach a certain proportion in a legislature, to the point at which they no longer feel like a few isolated individuals, their group solidarity increases and the pressure to conform to male norms decreases; the evidence tends to support this.[4] This critical mass effect is enhanced formally as larger numbers of women also are able to form effective women's caucuses.[5] The solidarity among women in a legislature may decline again as women in government become not only more numerous but also ideologically more diverse. Yet even in the 104th Congress (1995–1996), with fewer Democratic women and a larger number of conservative Republican women than any previous Congress, women tended to be more supportive than men of women's, children's, and family issues.[6]

Research on leadership behavior, furthermore, demonstrates that women more often than men exhibit an integrative leadership style that emphasizes cooperation and inclusiveness over competitive bargaining, and they more often seek community-based solutions over punitive solutions to problems.[7] There is evidence that as women's presence increases in legislatures, the men as well as the women adopt a more "female" or "feminist" leadership style, emphasizing outreach and consensus, as opposed to a more "masculine" style of command and control.[8]

Women in government represent women substantively as well as symbolically, and their increasing presence in government has broadened the reach and the legitimacy of American democracy. Women's PACs such as EMILY's List, The WISH List, and the Susan B. Anthony List facilitate the representative process by acting as intermediaries between constituents and representatives. The three women's PACs, like the female candidates they help to elect, are no more monolithic than the men who dominate American politics. The major contributors who support these women's PACs, demonstrating a wide divergence in political preferences and priorities, clearly do not see themselves as fighting in common cause. But in a world where men dominate both the candidate pool and the contributor pool, these women's PACs together are changing the gender imbalance in electoral politics.

NOTES

1. Michael B. Berkman and Robert E. O'Connor, "Do Women Legislators Matter? Female Legislators and State Abortion Policy," *American Politics Quarterly* 21 (1993), pp. 102–124; Debra L. Dodson, "Representing Women's Interests in the U.S. House of Representatives," in *Women and Elective Office: Past, Present, and Future,* ed. Sue Thomas and Clyde Wilcox (New York: Oxford University Press, 1998); Kathleen Dolan and Lynn Ford, "Women in the State Legislatures: Feminist Identity and Legislative Behaviors," *American Politics Quarterly* 23 (1995), pp. 96–108; Ruth B. Mandel and Debra L. Dodson, "Do Women Officeholders Make a Difference?" in *The American Woman, 1992–1993: A Status Report,* ed. Paula Ries and Anne J. Stone (New York: W. W. Norton, 1992); Michelle A. Saint-Germain, "Does Their Difference Make a Difference? The Impact of Women on Public Policy in the Arizona Legislature," *Social Science Quarterly* 70 (1989), pp. 856–968; Michele L. Swers, *The Difference Women Make: The Policy Impact of Women in Congress* (Chicago: University of Chicago Press, 2002); Karin L. Tamerius, "Sex, Gender, and Leadership in the Representation of Women," in *Gender, Power, Leadership, and Governance,* ed. Georgia Duerst-Lahti and Rita Mae Kelly (Ann Arbor, MI: University of Michigan Press, 1995); Sue Thomas, *How Women Legislate* (New York: Oxford University Press, 1994); Sue Thomas and Susan Welch, "The Impact of Gender on Activities and Priorities of State Legislatures," *Western Political Quarterly* 44 (1991), pp. 445–456.
2. Clara Bingham, *Women on the Hill: Challenging the Culture of Congress* (New York: Time Books, 1997); Susan J. Carroll, "Representing Women: Congresswomen's Perception of Their Representational Roles," in *Women Transforming Congress,* ed. Cindy Simon Rosenthal (Norman, OK: University of Oklahoma Press, 2002); Irwin Gertzog, *Congressional Women: Their Recruitment, Integration, and Behavior,* 2nd ed. (Westport, CT: Praeger, 1995); Beth Reingold, *Representing Women: Sex, Gender, and Legislative Behavior in Arizona and California* (Chapel Hill, NC: University of North Carolina Press, 2000); Swers, *The Difference Women Make;* Thomas, *How Women Legislate.*
3. John M. Carey, Richard G. Niemi, and Lynda W. Powell, "Are Women State Legislators Different?" in *Women and Elective Office: Past, Present, and Future,* ed. Sue Thomas and Clyde Wilcox (New York: Oxford University Press, 1998); Mandel and Dodson, "Do Women Officeholders Make a Difference?"; Thomas, *How Women Legislate.*
4. Berkman and O'Connor, "Do Women Legislators Matter?"; Saint-Germain, "Does Their Difference Make a Difference?"; Thomas, *How Women Legislate.*
5. Barbara C. Burrell, *A Woman's Place is in the House: Campaigning for Congress in the Feminist Era* (Ann Arbor, MI: University of Michigan Press, 1994); Mandel and Dodson, "Do Women Officeholders Make a Difference?"; Reingold, *Representing Women.*
6. Janet Clark, "Women at the National Level: An Update on Roll Call Voting Behavior," in *Women and Elective Office: Past, Present, and Future,* ed. Sue Thomas and Clyde Wilcox (New York: Oxford University Press, 1998); Swers, *The Difference Women Make.*

7. Lyn Kathlene, "Alternative Views of Crime: Legislative Policymaking in Gendered Terms," *Journal of Politics* 57 (1995), pp. 696–723; Cindy Simon Rosenthal, *When Women Lead: Integrative Leadership in State Legislatures* (New York: Oxford University Press, 1998); Michele L. Swers, "Research on Women in Legislatures: What Have We Learned, Where Are We Going?" *Women and Politics* 23 (2001), pp. 167–185.

8. Marcia Lynn Whicker and Malcolm Jewell, "The Feminization of Leadership in State Legislatures," in *Women and Elective Office: Past, Present, and Future,* ed. Sue Thomas and Clyde Wilcox (New York: Oxford University Press, 1998).

DATA COLLECTION

The original populations surveyed were persons who contributed $200 or more to The WISH List or EMILY's List during the 1996 election cycle. Since street addresses were stripped from the records of the two lists, it was necessary to go to the Federal Election Commission in Washington, D.C., to look them up for the mailing. The Federal Election Commission, which requires that all donations of $200 or more be reported by the organizations, with records made available to the public, provided the names and addresses of contributors. The two-wave survey was mailed in 1998 to the entire population of The WISH List contributors in FEC records and to an equivalent sample of the contributors to EMILY's List. The respondents to the 1998 survey were overwhelmingly female: 94 percent of EMILY's List contributors and 89 percent of The WISH List contributors.

From comments on our presentation of some early findings, we became interested in learning more about the male contributors and how they might compare to the women. Therefore, to expand the number of men in the analysis, a follow-up, two-wave survey was mailed to all of the men in the EMILY's List 1996 election cycle database. Because questionnaires were mailed to the entire population of EMILY's men, WISH women, and WISH men, but only to a sample of EMILY's women, EMILY's women in the final dataset were weighted by a factor of 19.12 to reflect their proportion of the population of EMILY's List contributors.

Surveys were mailed after the elimination of duplicate entries by combining the records of those who contributed more than once in the election cycle and after the elimination of records without street addresses. In 1998, we mailed surveys to 321 contributors to EMILY's List and to 224 contributors to The WISH List; 41 of the former and 25 of the latter were returned undeliverable. Eighty-eight questionnaires were returned completed from WISH List donors for a return rate of 44 percent. One hundred forty-seven were returned from EMILY's List for a return rate of 52 percent. In 1999, moreover, 422 surveys were mailed initially to the male contributors to EMILY's List.

Questionnaires were completed and returned by 153 male contributors to EMILY's List for a return rate of 36 percent.

For balance on the pro-choice/pro-life political debate, we expanded the research project in 2000 to contributors to the pro-life Susan B. Anthony List. As with the surveys of contributors to The WISH List and to EMILY's List, we did a two-wave mailing to 158 contributors to the Susan B. Anthony List, and we added a third wave in early 2001 due to the low response rate to the first two mailings. Twenty-two were returned undeliverable, reducing the number of potential respondents to 136. The three mailings resulted in fifty completed surveys from Susan B. Anthony List donors for a return rate of 37 percent.

The comparison of respondents with the entire samples in terms of variables in the FEC data—the total amount contributed and the state to which the questionnaire was mailed—shows the respondents to be representative of the sample as a whole as shown in Table A.1.

The questionnaires were identical except for the words "EMILY's," "WISH,"and "Susan B. Anthony" which corresponded to the respondent's organization with the exception of a question about vote choice in the 2000 election which was added to the Susan B. Anthony List questionnaire. The questionnaires covered partisanship and ideology, policy preferences and priorities, other political activities and organizational involvements, political efficacy and group feeling thermometers, and basic social/demographic characteristics. A reproduction of the questionnaire is shown in Appendix B.

TABLE A.1   COMPARISON OF CENSUS REGION AND REPORTED
FEC CONTRIBUTIONS FOR 1998 THE WISH LIST AND EMILY'S LIST AND FOR 2000
SUSAN B. ANTHONY LIST CONTRIBUTORS MAILED AND RETURNED SURVEYS

	SURVEY MAILING		RETURNED SURVEYS	
	N	%	N	%
Census Region[*]				
WISH List				
Northeast	78	34.8	27	30.7
North Central	22	9.8	9	10.2
South	70	31.3	29	33.0
West	54	24.1	23	26.1
	224	**100.0**	**88**	**100.0**
EMILY's List				
Northeast	88	27.4	38	25.9
North Central	47	14.6	30	20.4
South	95	29.6	37	25.2
West	91	28.3	42	28.6
	321	**99.9**	**147**	**100.1**
Anthony List				
Northeast	25	18.0	8	17.0
North Central	28	20.1	9	19.1
South	71	51.1	24	51.1
West	15	10.8	6	12.8
Don't Know[**]	0	—	3	—
	139	**100.0**	**50**	**100.0**
Reported Contributions				
WISH List				
Median	$1,000		$1,000	
Mean	1,336		1,473	
EMILY's List				
Median	$250		$250	
Mean	643		656	
Anthony List				
Median	$500		$430	
Mean	1,064		853	

[*]The states included in the respective census regions are: **Northeast** = CT, ME, MA, NH, NJ, NY, PA, RI, and VT; **North Central** = IL, IN, IA, KS, MI, MN, MO, NE, ND, OH, SD, and WI; **South** = AL, AR, DE, DC, FL, GA, KY, LA, MD, MS, NC, OK, SC, TN, TX, VA, and WV; **West** = AK, AZ, CA, CO, HI, ID, MT, NV, NM, OR, UT, WA, and WY.

[**]Three of the fifty respondents removed all identifying marks and returned their surveys in their own unmarked envelopes; thus, it was not possible to determine their state of origin.

Women's PAC Contributor Survey

This project is being conducted by researchers at the University of New Orleans. Your responses to the questions below are very important to us in understanding women's campaigns for elective office. All of your answers **WILL BE KEPT COMPLETELY CONFIDENTIAL** and will only be used in the aggregate. Neither the data nor any report on the data will be released in any form that permits identification of individual respondents. Thank you.

1. **First, a few questions about your involvement with [PAC Name].**
   1a. How many years have you contributed to candidates through [PAC Name]? _____
   1b. How many candidates have you contributed to through [PAC Name]?
   [ ] 1   [ ] 2–4   [ ] 5–9   [ ] 10–14   [ ] 15–19   [ ] 20 or more
   1c. How much money (in dollars) did you contribute during the 1995–1996 election cycle **[1997–1998 election cycle for Susan B. Anthony List contributors]** to:
   the [PAC Name] organization? $_____
   candidates recommended by [PAC Name]? $_____
   1d. What types of candidates have you contributed to through [PAC Name]? (Check all that apply)
   [ ] U.S. Congress
   [ ] Statewide office
   [ ] State legislature
   [ ] Other (specify) _____
   1e. How did you hear about [PAC Name] and decide to become involved?
   [ ] Mail from the organization
   [ ] Phone call from the organization
   [ ] Through a friend/acquaintance
   [ ] TV or radio
   [ ] World Wide Web
   [ ] Other (specify) _____

2. **Next, we would like to ask about your other political activities.**

    2a. During the past two years, did you ever (check all that apply):

    [ ] talk to any people and try to show them why they should vote
    for or against one of the parties or candidates?

    [ ] wear a campaign button, put a campaign sticker on your car, or
    place a campaign sign in your window or in front of your
    house?

    [ ] go to any political meetings, rallies, speeches, dinners, or things
    like that in support of a particular candidate?

    [ ] do any other work for one of the parties or candidates?

    [ ] give money to any candidates besides the contributions through
    [PAC Name]?

    [ ] give money to a political party?

    [ ] run for public office yourself?

    2b. We're also interested in what other kinds of organizations you
    might be involved with besides [PAC Name]. For each of the
    following types of organizations: (1) Are you a member? (2) In the
    past 12 months have you paid dues or given the organization any
    money? (3) In the past 12 months have you attended a meeting or
    taken part in any activities sponsored by the organization? (Check
    all that apply.)

Type of Organization	Member	Given Money / Paid Dues	Activity / Meeting
Women's rights group	[ ]	[ ]	[ ]
Pro-choice group	[ ]	[ ]	[ ]
Other political issue group	[ ]	[ ]	[ ]
Church or religious group	[ ]	[ ]	[ ]
Labor union	[ ]	[ ]	[ ]
Business or professional group	[ ]	[ ]	[ ]
Elderly organization	[ ]	[ ]	[ ]
Ethnic organization	[ ]	[ ]	[ ]
Civic or community group	[ ]	[ ]	[ ]
Children's organization	[ ]	[ ]	[ ]
Service organization	[ ]	[ ]	[ ]
Fraternal organization	[ ]	[ ]	[ ]
Educational or cultural group	[ ]	[ ]	[ ]
Self-help group	[ ]	[ ]	[ ]
Other type of group	[ ]	[ ]	[ ]

3. **Next, we would like to ask you some questions about your political views.**
   3a. What is your view concerning the following issues?
       (Circle 1 = Strongly Agree, 2 = Agree, 3 = Disagree, or
       4 = Strongly Disagree)

	STRONGLY AGREE	AGREE	DISAGREE	STRONGLY DISAGREE
The government in Washington should make every effort to improve the social and economic situation for women.	1	2	3	4
By law a woman should be able to obtain an abortion as a matter of personal choice.	1	2	3	4
Defense spending should be increased.	1	2	3	4
The government in Washington should reduce spending on domestic services, such as health and education, in order to cut the taxes paid by ordinary Americans.	1	2	3	4
Prayer should be allowed in the public schools.	1	2	3	4
The government in Washington should make every effort to improve the social and economic position of blacks and other minority groups.	1	2	3	4
The sale of handguns should be banned by law.	1	2	3	4
Government spending on improving and protecting the environment should be increased.	1	2	3	4
The government in Washington should see to it that every person has a job and a good standard of living.	1	2	3	4
Women should have an equal role with men in running business, industry, and government.	1	2	3	4
The government ought to help people get doctors and hospital care at low cost.	1	2	3	4
Because of past discrimination, blacks should be given preference in hiring and promotion.	1	2	3	4
In the future, the United States should be willing to use military force to solve international problems.	1	2	3	4
The government should pass and enforce laws protecting homosexuals from job discrimination.	1	2	3	4
Persons convicted of murder should be subject to the death penalty.	1	2	3	4
Mothers should remain at home with young children and not work outside the home.	1	2	3	4
The main reason government has become bigger over the years is because it has gotten involved in things that people should do for themselves.	1	2	3	4

3b. How important is each of the following issues in your decision of whether or not to support a political candidate? For each of the issues below, please indicate a rating from 1 (very important) to 5 (not at all important).

_____ Tax policy	_____ Stand on abortion
_____ Environmental policy	_____ Gender issues
_____ Health care policy	_____ Jobs
_____ National defense	_____ Race issues
_____ Stand on affirmative action	_____ AIDS policy
_____ Position on lesbian/gay rights	_____ Trade policy

3c. What do you think is the most important problem facing this country? _____

3d. What about your political beliefs? Do you consider yourself . . . ?

[ ] very liberal   [ ] somewhat conservative
[ ] somewhat liberal   [ ] very conservative
[ ] middle of the road/moderate

3e. Generally speaking, do you usually think of yourself as a Republican, a Democrat, an independent or what in **national** politics? In **state** politics?

NATIONAL POLITICS	STATE POLITICS
[ ] Strong Democrat	[ ] Strong Democrat
[ ] Weak Democrat	[ ] Weak Democrat
[ ] Independent but Lean Democratic	[ ] Independent but Lean Democratic
[ ] Independent	[ ] Independent
[ ] Independent but Lean Republican	[ ] Independent but Lean Republican
[ ] Weak Republican	[ ] Weak Republican
[ ] Strong Republican	[ ] Strong Republican
[ ] Other Party (Specify) _____	[ ] Other Party (Specify) _____

3e1. In the 2000 election for president, did you vote? **[Only for Susan B. Anthony List contributors.]**

[ ] Yes, voted for Bush	[ ] No, but favored Bush
[ ] Yes, voted for Gore	[ ] No, but favored Gore
[ ] Yes, voted for Nader	[ ] No, but favored Nader
[ ] Yes, voted for Buchanan	[ ] No, but favored Buchanan
[ ] Yes, voted for Browne	[ ] No, but favored Browne
[ ] Yes, voted for other candidate	[ ] No, but favored other candidate
	[ ] No, didn't like anybody

3f. In the 1996 election for president, did you vote?

[ ] Yes, voted for Clinton	[ ] No, but favored Clinton
[ ] Yes, voted for Dole	[ ] No, but favored Dole
[ ] Yes, voted for Perot	[ ] No, but favored Perot
[ ] Yes, voted for other candidate	[ ] No, but favored other candidate
	[ ] No, didn't like anybody

3g. Did you vote in the 1992 presidential election?

[ ] Yes, voted for Clinton   [ ] No, but favored Clinton
[ ] Yes, voted for Bush   [ ] No, but favored Bush
[ ] Yes, voted for Perot   [ ] No, but favored Perot
[ ] Yes, voted for other candidate [ ] No, but favored other candidate
                                    [ ] No, didn't like anybody

3h. Please indicate how you feel toward each of the following political leaders and groups by rating them on a thermometer that runs from 0 degrees to 100 degrees. Ratings between 50 degrees and 100 degrees mean that you feel favorable and warm toward the person or group. Ratings between 0 degrees and 50 degrees mean that you don't feel too favorable and are cool toward the person or group. You may use any number from 0 to 100 to indicate how favorable or unfavorable your feelings are for each person or group. Please indicate your feelings on the line provided.

_____ Bill Clinton   _____ People on welfare
_____ Environmentalists   _____ Older people
_____ Conservatives   _____ Christian fundamentalists
_____ Newt Gingrich   _____ Liberals
_____ Abortion opponents   _____ Republicans
_____ Labor unions   _____ Blacks
_____ Catholic church   _____ The military
_____ Federal government   _____ Lesbians/gays
_____ Women's movement   _____ Whites
_____ Big business   _____ Supporters of abortion
_____ Democrats

3i. For each of the following statements, please indicate your opinion.

	STRONGLY AGREE	AGREE	DISAGREE	STRONGLY DISAGREE
Generally speaking, the government in Washington can be trusted to do what is right.	1	2	3	4
People like me don't have any say about what the government does.	1	2	3	4
I don't think public officials care much about what people like me think.	1	2	3	4
Sometimes politics and government seem so complicated that a person like me can't really understand what's going on.	1	2	3	4
I feel that I have a pretty good understanding of the important political issues facing our country.	1	2	3	4

3j. Do you think of yourself as a feminist . . . ?
[ ] most of the time   [ ] some of the time   [ ] occasionally   [ ] never
3k. Do you think of yourself as a homemaker . . . ?
[ ] most of the time   [ ] some of the time   [ ] occasionally   [ ] never
3l. Do you think of yourself as a working woman/man . . . ?
[ ] most of the time   [ ] some of the time   [ ] occasionally   [ ] never

4. **Finally, we would like some information about your personal background.**
4a. In what state do you live? _____
4b. Which of the following best describes the community in which you live? (If you are a dependent student please indicate the type of community in which you grew up.)

[ ] A very large city (over 1,000,000)   [ ] A medium sized city (50,000–250,000)
[ ] A large city (250,000–1,000 000)   [ ] A small city or town (under 50,000)
[ ] A suburb near a large city   [ ] A farm or a farming community

4c. What is the highest level of schooling you have completed?

[ ] Completed grade school or less   [ ] 2-year college degree
[ ] Some high school   [ ] 4-year college degree
[ ] Completed high school   [ ] Some graduate or professional school
[ ] Some college   [ ] Graduate or professional school degree

4d. What is your current family status?

[ ] Married and living with spouse   [ ] Divorced/no longer living with partner
[ ] Living with a partner   [ ] Separated from spouse/partner
[ ] Widowed/survivor of partner   [ ] Single (never married/never lived with partner)

4e. Do you have any children?
[ ] Yes—please indicate their ages _____
[ ] No
4f. In what year were you born? _____
4g. What is your sex?
[ ] Female   [ ] Male
4h. How do you describe yourself? Please indicate your ethnic heritage/national origin.

[ ] Asian American   [ ] Native American/American Indian
[ ] Black/African American   [ ] White/Caucasian
[ ] Hispanic/Latino(a)   [ ] Other _____

4i. What is your sexual orientation?
[ ] Lesbian/gay   [ ] Heterosexual
[ ] Bisexual   [ ] Asexual

4j. What is your current employment status?
[ ] Working full-time   [ ] Temporarily laid-off
[ ] Temporarily disabled   [ ] Retired
[ ] Working part-time   [ ] Unemployed
[ ] Permanently disabled   [ ] Student
[ ] Full-time homemaker

4k. What is/was your occupation? _____

4l. What was your household income last year before taxes? (If you are a dependent student, please indicate your family's income.)
[ ] Under $10,000   [ ] $50,000–$59,999
[ ] $10,000–$19,999   [ ] $60,000–$69,999
[ ] $20,000–$29,999   [ ] $70,000–$80,000
[ ] $30,000–$39,999   [ ] over $80,000
[ ] $40,000–$49,999

4m. What was your personal income last year before taxes?
[ ] Under $10,000   [ ] $50,000–$59,999
[ ] $10,000–$19,999   [ ] $60,000–$69,999
[ ] $20,000–$29,999   [ ] $70,000–$80,000
[ ] $30,000–$39,999   [ ] over $80,000
[ ] $40,000–$49,999

4n. What, if any, is your religious preference?
[ ] Protestant (church or denomination? _____
[ ] Roman Catholic
[ ] Jewish
[ ] Other _____
[ ] None

4o. Would you say you go to church/synagogue . . . ?
[ ] once a week, or more   [ ] once or twice a month
[ ] almost every week   [ ] a few times a year
[ ] almost never

4p. In describing yourself religiously to others would you use any of the following descriptions? IF SO, please mark those that are appropriate:
[ ] Charismatic   [ ] Born Again
[ ] Fundamentalist   [ ] None of them
[ ] Evangelical

4q. Do you agree or disagree with the statement: "The Bible is God's word and all it says is true"?
[ ] Agree   [ ] Disagree

5.   **Additional comments about this survey or about women in politics.**

_____

_____

_____

_____

_____

_____

_____

_____

_____

_____

Thank you very much! Please put this form in the prepaid envelope and drop it in the mail.

If you would like a copy of the report summarizing the results of this survey, please print your name and address below:

_____
Name

_____
Address

_____

_____
                                                    Zip Code

Wording of National Election Study (NES) Questions

Political Efficacy

People like me don't have any say about what the government does. [5-point scale.]

Public officials don't care much what people like me think. [5-point scale.]

Sometimes politics and government seem so complicated that a person like me can't really understand what's going on. [5-point scale.]

Political Activities

During the campaign, did you ever:

talk to any people and try to show them why they should vote for or against one of the parties or candidates?

wear a campaign button, put a campaign sticker on your car, or place a campaign sign in your window or in front of your house?

go to any political meetings, rallies, speeches, dinners, or things like that in support of a particular candidate?

do any other work for one of the parties or candidates?

give money to any candidates?

give money to a political party?

give money to any other group that supported or opposed candidates?

Political Issues

Recently there has been a lot of talk about women's rights. Some people feel that women should have an equal role with men in running business, industry, and government. Others feel that a woman's place is in the home. [7-point scale]

Mothers should remain at home and not work. [5-point scale]

[Choose one] 1. By law, abortion should never be permitted. 2. The law should permit abortion only in cases of rape, incest, or when the woman's life is in danger. 3. The law should permit abortion for reasons other than rape, incest, or when the woman's life is in danger, but only after the need for abortion has been clearly established. 4. By law a woman should be able to obtain an abortion as a matter of personal choice.

Some people believe that we should spend much less money for defense. Others feel that defense spending should be greatly increased. [7-point scale]

Do you favor cuts in spending on domestic programs like Medicare, education, and highways in order to cut the taxes paid by ordinary Americans? [2-point scale]

[Choose one] 1. By law, prayer should not be allowed in public schools. 2. The law should allow public schools to schedule time when children can pray silently if they want to. 3. The law should allow public schools to schedule time when children as a group can say a general prayer not tied to a particular religious faith. 4. By law, public schools should schedule a time when all children would say a chosen Christian prayer.

Some people feel that the government in Washington should make every effort to improve the social and economic position of blacks. Others feel that the government should not make any special effort to help blacks because they should help themselves. [7-point scale]

Do you favor or oppose a ban on the sale of all handguns, except those that are issued to law enforcement officers? [2-point scale]

Some people feel the government in Washington should see to it that every person has a job and a good standard of living. Others think the government should just let each person get ahead on their own. [7-point scale]

There is much concern about the rapid rise in medical and hospital costs. Some people feel there should be a government insurance plan which would cover all medical and hospital expenses for everyone. Others feel that all medical expenses should be paid by individuals and through private insurance plans like Blue Cross or some other company paid plans. [7-point scale]

Some people feel that because of past discrimination, blacks should be given preference in hiring and promotion. Others say that such preferences in hiring and promotion of blacks is wrong because it gives blacks advantages they haven't earned. [2-point scale]

Do you favor or oppose laws to protect homosexuals against job discrimination? [2-point scale]

Do you favor or oppose the death penalty for persons convicted of murder? [2-point scale]

INDEX